# THE HOSTAGE

First staged by Joan Littlewood at the Theatre
Royal, Stratford in 1958, this play is about a
young Cockney soldier held as a hostage in a
Dublin lodging house for an I.R.A. man who is
to be hanged in Belfast. He is accidentally shot
in a raid on the house by Civic Guards. As well
as being a witty and often profound comment on
Anglo-Irish relations and on the Irish themselves, it is also a magnificent entertainment
which is full of rollicking comedy diversified by
ballads, satirical songs and dancing.

Kenneth Tynan in the *Observer* said of this
play: "It seems to be Ireland's function, every
twenty years or so, to provide a playwright who
will kick English drama from the past into
the present. Mr. Behan may well fill the place
vacated by Sean O'Casey."

*The photograph reproduced on the front of the cover is
of Murray Melvin as the Soldier; that on the back shows
Brendan Behan on the stage of the Theatre Royal,
Stratford, London. Both are by courtesy of Black
Star, London.*

D1027260

*By the same author*
THE QUARE FELLOW
BORSTAL BOY

# The Hostage

by

Brendan Behan

EYRE METHUEN LTD

LONDON

This play is fully protected by copyright. All inquiries concerning performing rights, professional or amateur, should be directed to Theatre Workshop, Theatre Royal, Stratford, London E.15

The text of this edition is that of the final version of the play as performed at Wyndham's Theatre.

The music for the play was arranged and edited by Kathleen O'Connor and can be obtained from the publishers, Chappell & Co. Ltd., 50 New Bond Street, London, W.1.

First published by Methuen & Co Ltd, 4 December 1958

Second edition (paperback) 1959

Reprinted twice 1960

Third edition, revised and reset, 1962

Reprinted six times

Reprinted 1973

© 1958 and 1962 by Theatre Workshop

Printed by Cox & Wyman Ltd, Fakenham, Norfolk

I.S.B.N. 0 413 31190 2

*"The Hostage" was first presented by Theatre Workshop at the Theatre Royal, Stratford, London E.15, on 14th October, 1958. A revised version was presented by Theatre Workshop at the Paris Théâtre des Nations Festival on 3rd April, 1959, and in conjunction with Donmar Productions Ltd., at Wyndham's Theatre on 11th June, 1959. The text in this edition is of this later production. The cast, on this occasion, was as follows:*

| | |
|---|---|
| PAT, *the caretaker of a lodging-house* | Howard Goorney |
| MEG DILLON, *his consort* | Eileen Kennally |
| MONSEWER, *the owner of the house* | Glynn Edwards |
| RIO RITA, *a homosexual navvy* | Stephen Cato |
| PRINCESS GRACE, *his coloured boy-friend* | Roy Barnett |
| MR. MULLEADY, *a decaying Civil Servant* | Brian Murphy |
| MISS GILCHRIST, *a social worker* | Ann Beach |
| COLETTE, *a whore* | Yootha Joyce |
| ROPEEN, *an old whore* | Leila Greenwood |
| LESLIE WILLIAMS, *a British soldier* | Alfred Lynch |
| TERESA, *the skivvy, a countrygirl* | Celia Salkeld |
| I.R.A. OFFICER, *a fanatical patriot* | James Booth |
| VOLUNTEER, *Feargus O'Connor, a ticket-collector* | Clive Barker |
| RUSSIAN SAILOR | Dudley Sutton |
| KATE, *the pianist* | Kathleen O'Connor |

The play produced by Joan Littlewood

Setting designed by Sean Kenny

# Act One

*The action of the play takes place in an old house in Dublin that has seen better days. A middle-aged man wearing carpet slippers, old corduroys and using a walking-stick is holding court. He runs the house. He doesn't own it, although he acts as though he does. This is because the real owner isn't right in his head and thinks he's still fighting in the Troubles or one of the anti-English campaigns before that.*

*Since the action of the play runs throughout the whole house and it isn't feasible to build it on stage, the setting is designed to represent one room of the house with a window overlooking the street. Leading off from this room are two doors and a staircase leading to the upper part. Between the room and the audience is an area that represents a corridor, a landing, or another room in the house and also serves as an extension of the room when the characters need room to dance and fight in.*

*The middle-aged man is* PATRICK, *an ex-hero and present-time brothel-keeper. During the first act of the play* PATRICK, *with the aid of* MEG DILLON, *his consort, is preparing the room that we can see, for a guest. It contains a table, two chairs and a brass bedstead. During the action of the play the other inhabitants of the house, in search of stout, physical comfort or the odd ballad, drift in and out of the room according to their curiosity and the state of* PAT's *temper. Like the house, they have seen better times. As the curtain rises, pimps, prostitutes, decayed gentlemen and their visiting "friends" are dancing a wild Irish jig, which is a good enough reason for* MEG *and* PAT *to stop their preparations and sit down for a drink of stout.*

1

*During the act these rests and drinks occupy more time than the actual work of preparation.*

*The jig reaches its climax and the dancers swing off the stage leaving* PAT *and* MEG *sitting at the table in the room.*

MEG. Thank God, that's over!

> *From the end of the passage comes the blast of an off-key bagpiper. The noise recedes into the distance.*

MEG. In the name of God, what's that?

PAT. It's Monsewer practising his music. He's taken it into his head to play the Dead March for the boy in Belfast Jail when they hang him in the morning. You know, the one that got copped for his I.R.A. activities.

MEG. I wish he'd kept it in his head. Those bagpipes get on me nerves.

PAT. Get us a drink.

MEG. Get it yourself.

PAT. I can't move my leg.

MEG. There's nothing wrong with your leg. [*She reaches him a bottle of stout.*] Here you are, you old scow.

> *A homosexual navvy,* RIO RITA, *attempts to get through the room and up the stairs without* PAT *seeing him. He is accompanied by a negro with a kit-bag.* PAT *spots them.*

PAT. Hey! Where's your rent?

RIO RITA. Give me a chance to earn it. [*They scuttle upstairs.*]

MEG. Do you think they will hang him?

PAT. Who, him? [*He indicates* RIO RITA'S *disappearing backside.*] They bloody well ought to!

MEG. No, the boy in Belfast Jail.

PAT. There's no think about it. Tomorrow morning at the hour of eight, he'll hang as high as Killymanjaro.

MEG. What the hell's that?

PAT. It's a noted mountain off the south coast of Switzerland. It would do you no good to be hung as high as that, anyway.

MEG. Do you know what he said? "As a soldier of the Irish Republic, I will die smiling."

PAT. And who asked him to give himself the trouble?

MEG. He only did his duty as a member of the I.R.A.

PAT. Don't have me use a coarse expression, you silly old bitch. This is nineteen-sixty, and the days of the heroes are over this forty years past. Long over, finished and done with. The I.R.A. and the War of Independence are as dead as the Charleston.

MEG. The old cause is never dead. "Till Ireland shall be free from the centre to the sea. Hurrah for liberty, says the Shan Van Vocht."

PAT. [*To the audience*] She's as bad as that old idiot out there. [*He indicates* MONSEWER.] It's bad enough he hasn't got a clock, but I declare to Jesus, I don't think he even has a calendar. And who has the trouble of it all? Me! He wants to have the New I.R.A., so-called, in this place now. Prepare a room for them, no less.

> COLETTE, *an attractive young whore, enters propelling a* SAILOR *before her. The* SAILOR *obviously speaks no English or Gaelic, and seeing the bed in the room starts to take his trousers off.* COLETTE *drags him away upstairs.*

COLETTE. I've got a right one here, this time. [*They go upstairs.*]

PAT. It's bad enough trying to run this place as a speak-easy and a brockel—

MEG. A what?

PAT. A brockel. That's English for whorehouse.

MEG. I will be thankful to you to keep that kind of talk about whorehouses to yourself. I'm no whore for one.

PAT. Why? Are you losing your union card?

*The* SAILOR *sings lustily upstairs.*

MEG. Well, if I'm a whore itself, you don't mind taking the best part of my money. So you're nothing but a ponce.

PAT. Well, I'm saving up to be one. And a long time that will take me with the money you can earn.

MEG. Well, you know what you can do. And shut that bloody row up there.

COLETTE [*off*]. And you.

PAT [*to* MEG]. You ought to know better than to abuse a poor crippled man that lost his leg, three miles outside of Mullingar.

MEG. There's nothing the matter with your leg.

PAT. And how do you think we could keep the house going on what we get from Monsewer? And who would look after him in England or Ireland if I didn't?

MEG. Not me for one.

PAT. Well, I'll stick by him because we were soldiers of Ireland in the old days.

*There is a* PIANIST *at one end of the passage area with the piano half on stage and half off.* PAT *signals to her and he sings:*

> On the Eighteenth day of November,
> Just outside the town of Macroom.,
> The Tans in their big Crossley tenders,
> Came roaring along to their doom.
> But the boys of the column were waiting
> With hand grenades primed on the spot,
> And the Irish Republican Army
> Made shit of the whole mucking lot

*The foreign* SAILOR *sings on.*

RIO RITA. Oh shut up, you dirty foreign bastard.
*Whilst* PAT *is singing all the other inhabitants come on to the stage, join in the song, and stay for a drink.*

MEG. You stand there singing about them ould times and the five glorious years, and yet you sneer and jeer at the boys of today. What's the difference.

PAT. It's the H bomb. It's such a big bomb it's got me scared of the little bombs. The I.R.A. is out of date—

ALL. Shame. No.

PAT.—and so is the R.A.F., the Swiss Guards, the Foreign Legion, the Red Army—

SAILOR. Niet.

PAT. —the United States Marines, the Free State Army, the Coldstream Guards, the Scots Guards, the Welsh Guards, the Grenadier Guards and the bloody fire guards.

MEG. Not the Horse Guards?

*A blast on the bagpipes and* MONSEWER *enters along the passage looking like Baden Powell in an Irish kilt and*

*flowing cloak. The noise from the bagpipes is terrible.*
*Everyone but* MEG *springs smartly to attention as* MON-
SEWER *passes and salutes.* MONSEWER *lives in a world*
*of his own, peopled by heroes and enemies. He spends*
*his time making plans for battles fought long ago*
*against enemies long since dead.*

MONSEWER [*greets him in Gaelic*]. Cén caoi ina bfuil tu.

PAT. Commandant-General.

MONSEWER. As you were, Patrick.

PAT. Thank you, Monsewer.

> PAT *stands at ease. The rest, except for Meg, drift away.*
> MONSEWER *addresses* PAT *with a great show of secrecy.*

MONSEWER. Patrick—preparations.

PAT. Everything's ready for the guest.

MONSEWER. Good, good. The troops will be coming quite
soon.

PAT [*aside*]. The troops! Good God! [*To* MONSEWER]. How
many of them are expected, then?

MONSEWER. There will be the two guards and the prisoner.

PAT. The prisoner?

MONSEWER. Yes. Yes, we only have the one at the moment,
but it's a good beginning.

PAT. Yes, indeed, as the Scotchman says, "Many a mickle
makes a muckle."

MONSEWER. And as we Irish say, "It's one after another
they built the castle. Iss in yeeg a Kale-ah shah togeock
nuh cashlawn."

PAT [*To the audience*]. Do you hear that? That's Irish. It's a
great thing, an Oxford University education! Me, I'm

only a poor ignorant Dublin man. I wouldn't understand a word of it. [*To* MONSEWER.] About this prisoner, Monsewer.

MONSEWER. Yes. An English laddie to be captured on the Border.

PAT. Armagh?

MONSEWER. Only one at first, but soon we'll have scores of them.

PAT [*aside*]. I hope to God he's not going to bring them all here.

MONSEWER. What's that?

PAT. I say, it's a great thing, the boys being out again sir.

MONSEWER. Absolutely first-class. Carry on.

> MONSEWER *marches off to make more plans.* PAT *retires defeated to have another stout.*

MEG. He's a decent old skin, even if he has got a slate loose.

PAT. Did you hear that? It's bad enough turning this place into an I.R.A. barracks. Monsewer wants to make a glass-house out of it now.

MEG. A what?

PAT. A kind of private Shepton Mallet of his own.

MEG. We should be proud to help the men that are fighting for Ireland. Especially that poor boy to be hanged in Belfast Jail tomorrow morning.

PAT. Why are you getting so upset over Ireland? Where the hell were you in nineteen-sixteen when the real fighting was going on?

MEG. I wasn't born yet.

PAT. You're full of excuses. Where were you when we had to go out and capture our own stuff off of the British Army?

MEG. Capture it? You told me that you bought it off the Tommies in the pub. You said yourself you got a revolver, two hundred rounds of ammunition, and a pair of jodhpurs off a colonel's batman for two pints of Bass and fifty Woodbines.

PAT. I shouldn't have given him anything. But I was sorry for him.

MEG. Why?

PAT. He got my sister in the family way.

MEG. Well, she was a dirty no-good. . .

*The conversation is interrupted by the rush of feet on the stairs. The* SAILOR *enters, minus his trousers, pursued by* COLETTE *in a dressing gown. The rear is brought up by* MR. MULLEADY, *a decaying Civil Servant. The row brings the other people in and the* SAILOR *is chased into a corner, where a menacing ring of people surrounds him.*

MULLEADY. Mr. Pat, Mr. Pat, that man, he—he's a Russian.

PAT. A what?

MULLEADY. A Russian.

PAT. Well, is he dirty or something?

MULLEADY. He's a Communist.

MEG. A Communist.

COLETTE. Oh now Pat, it's against my religion to have anything to do with the likes of him.

PAT. You have to pick up trade where you can these days. The only reason I know for throwing a man out is when he has no money to pay.

MEG. Has he got any?

PAT. I'll find out. Have you got any money? Any gelt? Dollars? Pound notes? Money? [PAT *makes a sign for money.*]

SAILOR. Da! Da! [*He produces a big wad of notes.*]

MEG. Do you see the wad he has on him? [*The* SAILOR *throws the money in the air and beams. They all dive for the money.*]

MEG. Sure, pound notes is the best religion in the world.

PAT. And the best politics, too.

*As they all scrabble and fight for the money on the floor, a voice thunders from the stairs:*

MONSEWER.      Hark a voice like thunder spake,
The west awake, the west awake.
Sing Oh Hurrah, for Ireland's sake,
Let England quake.

SAILOR. Mir y drushva!

MONSEWER. Cén caoi ina bfuil tu. (*He compliments* COLETTE] Carry on, my dear. Ireland needs the work of the women as well, you know. [*Exit.*]

COLETTE. Is it all right now?

PAT. Yes, go on.

COLETTE. Well, I've been to confession three times already and I don't want to make a mistake about it.

COLETTE *takes the* RUSSIAN SAILOR *upstairs to bed. The excitement over, everyone drifts off, leaving* MR. MULLEADY *with* PAT *and* MEG.

MULLEADY. I'm sorry, Mrs. M.—I mean about the Russian. I felt that as a God-fearing man I could shut my eyes no longer.

MEG. Anybody would think you was doing God a good turn speaking well of him.

MULLEADY. Oh, and another thing—about my laundry, Miss Meg. It was due back three days ago.

PAT. It walked back.

MULLEADY. I have to go to one of my committees this evening and I haven't a shirt to my name.

MEG. Go and ask the Prisoners Aid Society to give you one.

MULLEADY. You know very well that is the committee on which I serve.

MEG. Well, go and wash one.

MULLEADY. You know I can't—

MEG. Get going, or I'll ask you for the money you owe me.

MULLEADY. Please don't bring all that up again. You know that at the end of the month . . .

MEG. Are you going? [*She drives him out.*] Fine thing to be letting rooms to every class of gouger and bowsey in the city.

PAT. Dirty thieves and whores the lot of them. Still, their money is clean enough.

MEG. It's not the whores I mind, it's the likes of that old whited sepulchre that I don't like.

> MULLEADY *comes downstairs with a filthy shirt and scoots through the room and out of the kitchen door.*

PAT. You don't mean Monsewer?

MEG. No, I don't. I mean that old Mulleady geezer, though Monsewer is bad enough, giving out about the Republic and living in a brockel.

PAT [*hushing her*]. Monsewer doesn't know anything about these matters.

MEG. Course he does, Pat.

PAT. He doesn't.

MEG. He must know.

PAT. No. He thinks everybody in this house are gaels, patriots or Republicans on the run.

MEG. He doesn't, the old idiot! He's here again.

> MONSEWER *enters, on secret service, carrying a sheaf of despatches and plans.*

MONSEWER. Patrick!

PAT. Sir!

MONSEWER. As you were. [PAT *stands at ease.*]

PAT. Thank you, Monsewer.

MONSEWER [*in great confidence*]. Patrick, I trust we may rely on the lads in the billet if anything should go wrong tonight?

PAT. We may put our lives in their hands, Monsewer.

MEG. God help us.

MONSEWER. There was a bit of a rumpus in here a minute ago, wasn't there?

PAT. Strain of battle, Commandant.

MONSEWER. Yes, yes. The boys are bound to be a bit restless on a night like this. It's in the air, Patrick—can you smell it? [*Like Wellington on the eve of Waterloo,* PAT *sniffs.*]

PAT. No, sir, I'm afraid I can't.

MONSEWER. The coming battle. I think you should have a copy of this, Patrick. Battle orders. Plenty of fodder in?

PAT. For the horses, Commandant?

MONSEWER. For the men, damn you! The men.

PAT. Oh yes, Monsewer. This is in Irish, Monsewer.

B

MONSEWER. At a time like this, we should refuse to use the English language altogether. [MONSEWER *surveys his imaginary battlefield, planning how he will deploy his forces.*]

PAT. Well, you've done your bit on that score, Monsewer. For years Monsewer wouldn't speak anything but Irish.

MEG. Most people wouldn't know what he was saying, surely.

PAT. No, they didn't. When he went on a tram or a bus he had to have an interpreter with him so the conductor would know where he wanted to get off.

MEG. Ah, the poor man.

MONSEWER. Patrick. [*He draws him aside.*] Any letters arrived for me from England lately?

PAT. No, sir.

MONSEWER. Oh dear. I was relying on my allowance for a few necessities.

PAT. Ah, never mind, sir, we'll keep the kip going somehow.

MEG. [*to the audience*]. Sure, he hasn't had a letter from England since they naturalised the Suez Canal.

MONSEWER. There's another matter: fellow patriot of ours calls himself Pig-eye—code name, of course. Just served six months in prison for the cause. I told him that, in return, he shall billet here, at our expense, till the end of his days. Carry on. [MONSEWER *marches off.*]

PAT [*to the Audience*]. Pig-eye! He's just done six months for robbery with violence. "Till the end of his days." If he doesn't pay his rent, he'll reach the end of his days sooner than he expects.

MEG. Don't you talk to me about that Pig-eye. He's as mean as the grave. A hundred gross of nylons he knocked off the other day, from the Hauty Cotture warehouse, and not one did he offer to a girl in the street. No bejasus, not even to the one legged-girl in Number 8. The old hypocrite.

PAT. Who? Pig-eye?

MEG. No. Monsewer. He's not as green as he's cabbage looking. Calling himself "Monsewer", blowing the head off you with his ould pipes, and not a penny to his name.

PAT. Well, he's loyal to the old cause, and he's a decent old skin.

> *As* PAT *begins to tell his story other people from the house edge in:* KATE, *the pianist,* RIO RITA *in a faded silk dressing-gown, and his coloured boy-friend,* MR. MULLEADY, COLETTE, *and the* SAILOR *and* OLD ROPEEN, *a retired whore. They egg* PAT *on or mock him, if they dare.*

MEG. Where did he get that monniker for a start? Is it an English name?

PAT. What?

MEG. Monsewer.

PAT. It's French for mister, isn't it?

MEG. I don't know. I'm asking you.

PAT. Well, I'm telling you, it is. At one time all the toffs were going mad, talking Irish and only calling themselves by their Irish names.

MEG. You just said it was a French name.

PAT. Will you let me finish for once? What's the Irish for mister?

ROPEEN. R. Goine Vasal.

> MEG *starts laughing.*

PAT. Yes, well it was too Irish for them, too, so they called themselves Monsieur or Madame as the case might be.

MEG. Ah, they're half mad, these high-up ould ones.

PAT. He wasn't half mad the first time I saw him, nor a quarter mad, God bless him. See that? [*He produces a photo.*] Monsewer on the back of his white horse, the Cross of Christ held high in his right hand, like Brian Boru, leading his men to war and glory.

MEG. Will you look at the poor horse.

PAT. That was the day we got captured. We could have got out of it, but Monsewer is terrible strict and honest. You see, he's an Englishman.

MEG. An Englishman, and him going round in a kilt all day playing his big Gaelic pipes.

PAT. He was born an Englishman, remained one for years. His father was a bishop.

MEG. His father was a bishop. [*All good Catholics, they start to leave.*] Well, I'm not sitting here and listening to that class of immoral talk. His father was a bishop, indeed!

PAT. He was a Protestant bishop.

MEG. Ah well, it's different for them. [*They all come back.*]

RIO RITA. They get married, too, sometimes.

PAT. He went to all the biggest colleges in England and slept in the one room with the King of England's son.

MEG. Begad, it wouldn't surprise me if he slept in the one bed with him, his father being a bishop.

PAT. Yes, he had every class of comfort, mixed with dukes, marquises, earls and lords.

MEG. All sleeping in the one room, I suppose?

ROPEEN. In the one bed.

PAT. Will you shut up. As I was saying, he had every class of comfort until one day he discovered he was an Irishman.

MEG. Aren't you after telling me he was an Englishman?

PAT. He was an Anglo-Irishman.

MEG. In the name of God, what's that?

PAT. A Protestant with a horse.

ROPEEN. Leadbetter.

PAT. No, no, an ordinary Protestant like Leadbetter, the plumber in the back parlour next door, won't do, nor a Belfast orangeman, not if he was as black as your boot.

MEG. Why not?

PAT. Because they work. An Anglo-Irishman only works at riding horses, drinking whisky and reading double-meaning books in Irish at Trinity College.

MEG. I'm with you he wasn't born an Irishman. He became one.

PAT. He didn't become one—he was born one—on his mother's side, and as he didn't like his father much he went with his mother's people—he became an Irishman.

MEG. How did he do that?

PAT. Well, he took it easy at first, wore a kilt, played Gaelic football on Blackheath.

MEG. Where's that?

PAT. In London. He took a correspondence course in the Irish language. And when the Rising took place he acted like a true Irish hero.

MEG. He came over to live in Ireland.

PAT. He fought for Ireland with me at his side,.

MEG. Aye, we've heard that part of the story before.

PAT. Five years' hard fighting.

COLETTE. Ah, God help us.

ROPEEN. Heavy and many is the good man that was killed.

PAT. We had the victory—till they signed that curse-of-God treaty in London. They sold the six counties to England and Irishmen were forced to swear an oath of allegiance to the British Crown.

MEG. I don't know about the six counties, but the swearing wouldn't come so hard on you.

ROPEEN. Whatever made them do it, Mr. Pat?

PAT. Well, I'll tell you, Ropeen. It was Lloyd George and Birkenhead made a fool of Michael Collins and he signed an agreement to have no more fighting with England.

MEG. Then he should have been shot.

PAT. He was.

MEG. Ah, the poor man.

PAT. Still, he was a great fighter and he fought well for the ould cause.

ROPEEN. They called him "The Laughing Boy".

PAT. They did.

RIO RITA. Give us your song, Pat. [*General agreement.*]

PAT. Give us a note. Kate.

> PAT *sings the first verse and the others join in, naturally, as they feel moved, into the choruses and the following verses.*

'Twas on an August morning, all in the morning hours,
I went to take the warming air all in the month of flowers,
And there I saw a maiden and heard her mournful cry,
Oh, what will mend my broken heart, I've lost my Laughing Boy.

MEG. So strong, so wide, so brave he was, I'll mourn his loss
  too sore
 When thinking that we'll hear the laugh or springing step
  no more.

ALL. Ah, curse the time, and sad the loss my heart to crucify,
  Than an Irish son, with a rebel gun, shot down my
   Laughing Boy.
  Oh, had he died by Pearse's side, or in the G.P.O.,
  Killed by an English bullet from the rifle of the foe,
  Or forcibly fed while Ashe lay dead in the dungeons of
   Mountjoy,
  I'd have cried with pride at the way he died, my own dear
   Laughing Boy.

RIO RITA. Now one voice.

MEG. My princely love, can ageless love do more than tell
  to you
 Go raibh mile maith Agath, for all you tried to do,
 For all you did and would have done, my enemies to
  destroy,

ALL. I'll praise your name and guard your fame, my own
  dear Laughing Boy.

PAT. It's a great story.

MEG. It's better than that show that used to be on the tele-
vision below in Tom English's Eagle Bar, "This is your
life".

PAT. It wasn't the end of the story. Some of us wouldn't
accept the treaty. We went on fighting, but we were beat.
Monsewer was loyal to the old cause and I was loyal to
Monsewer. So when the fighting was done we came back
together to this old house.

MEG. This dirty old hole.

PAT. A good hole it was for many a decent man on the run for twenty years after that.

MEG. Who the hell was still running twenty years after that?

PAT. All the Republicans who wouldn't accept the Treaty. We put Cosgrave's government in and he had the police hunting us.

RIO RITA. Then you put de Valera in, and he started hunting us too.

PAT. I put de Valera in—what the hell are you talking about?

RIO RITA. I ought to know what I'm talking about—I was Michael Collins's runner in the old days.

PAT. He must have had a thousand bloody runners if you were another one.

RIO RITA. Are you calling me a liar?

PAT. Oh get out.

RIO RITA. You know I was Michael Collins's runner.

MULLEADY. That was over thirty years ago—you weren't even born.

RIO RITA. I did my bit in O'Connell Street, with the rest of them.

ROPEEN. He did his bit up in O'Connell Street.

RIO RITA. You shut your bloody row—you want to take a bucket of water out with you when you go out the back, you do.

ROPEEN. Get out, will you. [*She chases him upstairs.*]

RIO RITA. There you are—look—she's picking on me again. I haven't said a word to her. I won't argue with her—I only upset meself if I argue with that one. I'll go and have a lie down. [*Exits.*]

MEG. Carry on with the coffin, the corpse'll walk.

PAT. Hiding hunted Republicans was all very well, but it didn't pay the rent, so in the end we had to take in all sorts of scruffy lumpers to make the place pay.

RIO RITA [*from the top of the stairs.*] You wouldn't say that to my face.

PAT. This noble old house, which housed so many heroes, was turned into a knocking shop. But I'd you to help me.

MEG. You had me to help you! The curse of God meet and melt you and your rotten lousy leg. You had me to help you, indeed! If I'm a whore itself, sure I'm a true patriot.

PAT. Course you are, course you are. Aren't we husband and wife—nearly?

MEG. Well, nearly.

PAT. Sure, I wasn't referring to you. I was talking about old Ropeen and that musician, and Colette, there's another one.

COLETTE. I don't have to stay here.

MEG. Don't you talk to me about that Colette, not after what she done to the poor old Civil Servant out of the Ministry of Pensions.

PAT. Never mind that now.

MEG. There was the poor old feller kneeling by the bedside saying his prayers. For Colette to go robbing him of all his money and him in the presence of Almighty God, so to speak.

*The sound of hymn-singing comes from upstairs. Down the stairs* RIO RITA *flies into the room, followed by the* NEGRO, *now in boxing kit with gloves on. The other people in the house flood into the room and listen to the din.*

What the hell's that? What's going on?

RIO RITA *silences the room and tells his story.*

RIO RITA. I've seen everything, dear. I've seen everything. I was upstairs doing a bit of shadow boxing with my friend.

MEG. Where the hell's that row coming from?

RIO RITA. It's that man in the third floor back. He has a strange woman in his room.

MEG. Old Mulleady?

RIO RITA. Three hours he's had her in there, and the noises, it's disgusting. It's all very well you laughing, but it doesn't say much for the rest of us girls in the house.

ROPEEN. No, it doesn't, does it?

MEG. Has he got that one-legged girl from Number 8 in there?

RIO RITA. No, she's not even out of the street, let alone the house. A complete stranger—I don't know the woman.

MEG. Well, what sort of woman is it?

RIO RITA. A female woman.

MEG. Well, the dirty low degenerate old maniac, what does he take this house for?

COLETTE. They're coming.

> MR. MULLEADY *and* MISS GILCHRIST *appear on the stairs kneeling and singing their prayers. Their shoes are beside them.*

MULLEADY. Let us say a prayer, Miss Gilchrist, and we will be forgiven. [MR. MULLEADY's *hand strays and gooses* MISS GILCHRIST.]

MISS GILCHRIST. In nomine—please, Mr. Mulleady, let us not fall from grace again.

MULLEADY. I'm very sorry, Miss Gilchrist, let not the right hand know what the left hand is doing. Miss Gilchrist, can you— [*The hand strays again and strokes* MISS GILCHRIST'S *tail*.]

MEG [*calling*]. Mr. Mulleady.

MULLEADY. —feel our souls together?

MEG. Mr. Mulleady.

> *The praying and the stroking stop.* MR. MULLEADY *puts on his shoes,* MISS GILCHRIST *smoothes her hair and dress. She looks very prim and proper.*

MULLEADY. Is that you, Mrs. M.?

MEG. Is it me? Who the hell do you think it is? Will you come down here and bring that shameless bitch down with you.

MULLEADY. What do you want? Did you call me, Mrs. M.?

MEG. If Mulleady is your name, I called you, and I called that low whore you have up there with you. I didn't call her by her name, for I don't know what it is, if she's got one at all. Come down from there, you whore, whoever you are.

> MEG *shoos everyone out of the room and hides behind the door.* MULLEADY *enters, sees no one and turns to go, only to find* MEG *blocking his path. She thrusts her bosom at him and drives him back on to one of the chairs.*

MULLEADY. Mrs. M., she might have heard you.

MEG. Who's she when she's at home, and what's she got that I haven't got, I should like to know.

MULLEADY. She is a lady.

MEG. The more shame to her, and don't you go calling me
　your dear Mrs. M. Nor your cheap Mrs. M. either. What
　do you mean by bringing whores into this house?

PAT. And it's full of them, coals to Newcastle.

> COLETTE, ROPEEN, RIO RITA *and* MEG *crowd* MULLEADY
> *and sit on his knees, ruffle his hair and tickle him.*
> *The* NEGRO *shadow boxes, the* SAILOR *falls asleep with*
> *a bottle of vodka and* PAT *takes no part in this.*

MEG. Now, Mr. Mulleady, Mr. Mulleady, sir, don't you
　know you could have got anything like that, that you
　wanted, here?

RIO RITA. Yes anything.

MEG. I'm surprised at you, so I am. God knows I've stuck
　by you. Even when that man there was wanting to cast
　you out into the streets for the low-down dirty old
　hypocrite that you are.

MULLEADY. Thank you, Mrs. M. Your blood's worth
　bottling.

MEG. Are you all right now?

MULLEADY. Oh yes, indeed, thank you.

MEG. Right then. Bring down that brassitute.

MULLEADY. Oh, is there any need?

MEG. Fetch her down.

MULLEADY [*feebly*]. Miss Gilchrist.

MEG. Louder.

MULLEADY. Miss Gilchrist.

MISS GILCHRIST. Yes, Mr. Mulleady?

MULLEADY. Will you come down here a minute, please.

MISS GILCHRIST. I haven't finished the first novena, Mr. Mulleady.

MEG. I'll give her the first bloody novena!

MULLEADY. Mrs. M., please. I'll get her down.

MR. MULLEADY *climbs the stairs and helps* MISS GILCHRIST *to her feet. Together they prepare to meet their martyrdom and they march resolutely down the stairs singing (to a corrupt version of Handel's Largo).*

MISS GILCHRIST
MULLEADY

We are soldiers of the Lord, Miss Gilchrist,
Forward to battle, forward side by side
Degenerates and lay-abouts cannot daunt us.
We are sterilized.

MISS GILCHRIST *takes a firm stand, whilst* MULLEADY *hands out religious tracts.*

MISS GILCHRIST. Save your souls, my brothers, my sisters, save your souls. One more sinner saved today. Jesus lives.

MULLEADY. This is Miss Gilchrist.

MEG. In the name of all that's holy, what kind of a name is Gilchrist.

MISS GILCHRIST. It is an old Irish name. In its original form "Giolla Christ", the servant or gilly of the Lord.

MEG. You're a quare-looking gilly of the lord, you whore.

MISS GILCHRIST. I take insults in the name of our blessed Saviour.

MEG. You take anything you can get like a good many more round here. You've been three hours up in his room.

MULLEADY. A quarter of an hour, Mrs. M.

ALL. Three hours.

MISS GILCHRIST. We were speaking of our souls.

MISS GILCHRIST⎫
MULLEADY    ⎬ [*singing*]. Our souls. Our souls. Our souls.

> [*This is slurred to sound*—"Our souls. Are souls. Arse-
> holes.]

MEG. You can leave his soul alone, whatever about your
own. And take yourself out of here, before I'm dug out
of you.

MISS GILCHRIST. I will give you my prayers.

MEG. You can stuff them up your cathedral.

MISS GILCHRIST. I forgive her. She is a poor sinful person.

MEG. And you're a half-time whore.

PAT. Compliments pass when the quality meet.

MISS GILCHRIST. Mr. Mulleady, come away. This is
Sodom and Gomorrah.

MEG [*stops him*]. Don't leave us, darlin'.

MULLEADY. I can't, Miss Gilchrist, I haven't paid my rent.

MISS GILCHRIST. I will pray for you, Eustace. My shoes,
please.

MULLEADY [*fetching her shoes*]. Will you come back, Miss
Gilchrist?

MISS GILCHRIST. The Lord will give me the strength. God
go with you.

> THE RUSSIAN SAILOR *goes to grab her. She runs out.*

MULLEADY. Evangelina!

PAT. Ships that pass in the night.

MEG. Did you ever see anything like that in you life before? Now are you going to ask for an explanation, or am I?

PAT. Leave me out of it. You brought him here in the first place.

MEG. So I did, God help me. And you can take your face out of here, you simpering little get.

MULLEADY *starts to go.*

Not you, him.

RIO RITA. Me—well there's gratitude for you. Who told you about him in the first place? I always knew what he was, the dirty old eye-box.

MULLEADY. Informer! Butterfly! You painted May-pole!

RIO RITA. You filthy old get!

PAT. Hey, what about some rent.

*The room clears as if by magic. Only* RIO RITA *is trapped on the stairs.*

RIO RITA. I wish you wouldn't show me up when I bring a friend into the house.

PAT. Never mind all that. What about the rent? What's his name, anyway?

RIO RITA. Princess Grace.

PAT. I can't put down Princess Grace, can I?

RIO RITA. That's only his name in religion.

MEG. Don't be giving out that talk about religion.

PAT. Well, what's his real name?

RIO RITA. King Kong. [*exit.*]

*A row erupts in the kitchen between* MULLEADY *and* ROPEEN *and* MULLEADY *enters, holding his dirty shirt.*

MULLEADY. Mr. Pat, Mr. Pat, she has no right to be in there all morning washing her aspidistra. I only wanted to wash my shirt. [*He recovers his dignity.*] All this fuss about Miss Gilchrist. She merely came to talk religion to me.

MEG. That is the worst kind. You can take it from me.

PAT. From one who knows.

MULLEADY. You don't seem aware of my antecedents. My second cousin was a Kilkenny from Kilcock.

MEG. I'll cock you. Take this broom and sweep out your room, you scowing little bollix—take it before I ruin you completely.

*She throws a broom at him and he disappears, flicking the old whore with the broom as he goes. Things quieten down and* PAT *and* MEG *take a rest.*

PAT. If the performance is over I'd like a cigarette.

MEG. I sent the skivvy out for them half an hour ago. God knows where she's got to. Have a gollywog.

PAT. What in the hell's name is that?

MEG. It's a French cigarette. I got them off that young attaché case at the French Embassy—that one that thinks all Irishwomen are his mother.

PAT. I don't fancy those. I'll wait for me twenty Afton. Meanwhile I'll sing that famous old song, "The Hound That Caught the Pubic Hair".

MEG. You're always announcing these songs, but you never get round to singing them.

PAT. Well, there is a song I sing sometimes.

> There's no place on earth like the world
> Just between you and me.
> There's no place on earth like the world,
> Acushla, astore and Mother Machree.

> TERESA, *the skivvy runs in. She is a strong hefty country girl of 19 and a bit shy.*

TERESA. Your cigarettes, sir.

PAT. A hundred thousand welcomes. You look lovely. If I wasn't married I'd be exploring you.

TERESA. I'm very sorry I was so late sir.

MEG. Were you lost in the place?

TERESA. I was, nearly. Shall I get on with the beds, Meg?

MEG. Yes, you might as well.

PAT. Don't be calling me sir, there's only one sir in this house and that's Monsewer. Just call me Pat.

TERESA. Pat, sir, there's a man outside.

MEG. Why doesn't he come in?

TERESA. Well, he's just looking around.

PAT. Is he a policeman?

TERESA. Oh no, sir, he looks respectable.

PAT. Where is he now? [TERESA *goes to the window.*]

TERESA. He's over there, sir.

PAT. I can't see without me glasses. Is he wearing a trench coat and a beret.

TERESA. He is, sir. How did you know!?

MEG. He's a fortune-teller.

TERESA. And he has a badge to say he only speaks Irish.

c

PAT. Begod, then him and me will have to use the deaf and
dumb language, for the only bit of Irish I know would get
us both prosecuted. That badge makes me think he's an
officer.

TERESA. He has another to say he doesn't drink.

PAT. That means he's a higher officer.

MEG. Begod, don't be bringing him in here.

PAT. He'll come in, in his own good time, Now, Teresa girl,
you haven't been here long but you're a good girl and
you can keep your mouth shut.

TERESA. Oh yes, sir.

PAT. Well, someone's coming to stay here and you'll bring
him his meals. Now, if you don't tell a living sinner about
it, you can stay here for the rest of your life.

MEG. Well, till she's married anyway.

TERESA. Thank you, sir. Indeed, I'm very happy here.

PAT. You're welcome.

TERESA. And I hope you'll be satisfied with my work.

PAT. I'd be more satisfied if you were a bit more cheerful
and not so serious all the time.

TERESA. I've always been a very serious girl.

*Sings:*

> Open the door softly,
> Shut it—keep out the draught,
> For years and years, I've shed millions of tears,
> And never but once have I laughed.
> 'Twas the time the holy picture fell,
>
> And knocked me old Granny cold,
> While she knitted and sang an old Irish song,
> 'Twas by traitors poor old Ulster was sold.

So open the window softly,
For Jaysus' sake, hang the latch,
Come in and lie down, and afterwards
You can ask me what's the catch.

Before these foreign-born bastards, dear,
See you don't let yourself down,
We'll be the Lion and Unicorn,
My Rose unto your Crown.

MEG. Hasn't she got a nice voice, Pat?

PAT. You make a pretty picture. Do you know what you look like, Meg?

MEG. Yes, a whore with a heart of gold. At least, that's what you'd say if you were drunk enough.

*Two men enter and begin examining the room, stamping on the boards, testing the plaster and measuring the walls. The first is a thin-faced fanatic in a trench coat and black beret. He is a part-time* OFFICER *in the* I.R.A. *The second man is* FEARGUS O'CONNOR, *a* VOLUNTEER. *He wears a rubber mackintosh and a shiny black cap. The* OFFICER *is really a schoolmaster and the* VOLUNTEER *a railway ticket-collector. They survey all exits and escape routes.*

RIO RITA. Is it the sanitary inspector, Pat?

OFFICER. Filthy—filthy. The whole place is filthy. [*He sees the* RUSSIAN SAILOR *asleep.*] Get rid of that, will you?

PAT. Who does this belong to?

COLETTE. That's mine.

RIO RITA. Let me give you a hand with him.

COLETTE. Keep your begrudging hands off him.
    COLETTE *exits with* SAILOR.

OFFICER. Who's in charge here?

PAT. I am.

OFFICER. Your cellar's full of rubbish.

PAT. Oh, there's no rubbish there. No, I'll tell you what there is in there. There's the contents of an entire house which nearly fell down a couple of weeks ago.

OFFICER. What are these people doing here?

PAT. Well, that's Meg and that's Teresa . . .

OFFICER. Get 'em out of here.

PAT. You'd better go—get out.

MEG. Come on, Teresa—if they want to play toy soldiers we'll leave them to it.

> *All leave except* PAT, I.R.A. OFFICER *and* VOLUNTEER. *The* VOLUNTEER *makes lists.*

OFFICER. You'll have to get that cellar cleared; it's an escape route.

PAT. Yes, sir.

OFFICER. Here's a list of your instructions; it's in triplicate, one for you, one for me and one for H.Q. When you've read and digested them, append your signature and destroy your copy. Do you have the Gaelic?

PAT. No, I'm afraid I don't.

OFFICER. Then we'll have to speak in English. Have you food sufficient for three people for one day?

PAT. There's always plenty of scoff in this house.

OFFICER. May I see your toilet arrangements, please?

PAT. Oh yes, just through that door—no, not that one—there. There's plenty of paper, and mind your head as you go in. [*The* OFFICER *goes.*]

MONSEWER [*off*]. I'm in here. [MONSEWER *comes out.*] No damned privacy in this house at all, Laddie from H.Q.?

PAT. Yes, sir.

MONSEWER. Damned ill-mannered. [*Exit. The* I.R.A. OFFICER *returns.*]

OFFICER. Who the hell was that?

PAT. My old mother.

OFFICER. Can we be serious, please?

PAT. Can I offer you any refreshment?

OFFICER. I neither eat nor drink when I'm on duty.

PAT. A bottle of stout?

OFFICER. Teetotal. I might take a bottle of orange and me after dancing the high caul cap in a Gaelic measurement at an Irish ceilidh, but not at any other time.

PAT. Well, no one would blame you for that.

OFFICER. Rent book, please.

PAT. Are you thinking of moving in?

OFFICER. I wish to see a list of tenants.

> PAT *takes out a very old dilapidated rent book.*

PAT. Well, there's Bobo, The Mouse, is Ropeen still here?— Mulleady. [*The people of the house look round the doors and whisper at* PAT.] Get out, will you? [*Goes back to book.*] Colette—ey, this one's been dead for weeks, I hope he's not still there. Rio Rita, Kate, Meg . . . Well, that's all I know about—there might be some more about some- where.

OFFICER. If it was my doings, there'd be no such thing as us coming here at all. And the filthy reputation this house has throughout the city.

PAT. Can't think how you came to hear about it at all, a clean-living man like yourself.

OFFICER. I do charitable work round here for the St. Vincent de Paul Society. Padraig Pearse said, "To serve a cause that is splendid and holy, the man himself must be splendid and holy."

PAT. Are you splendid, or just holy? Rent in advance, four pounds.

OFFICER. Is it money you're looking for?

PAT. We're not all working for St. Vincent de Paul.

OFFICER. Will you leave St. Vincent out of it, please.

PAT. Begod, and I will. [To the audience.] St. Vincent de Paul Society! They're all ex-policemen. In the old days we wouldn't go anywhere near them.

OFFICER. In the old days there were nothing but Communists in the I.R.A.

PAT. There were some. What of that?

OFFICER. Today the movement is purged of the old dross. It has found its spiritual strength.

PAT. Where did it find that?

OFFICER. "The man who is most loyal to the faith is the one who is most loyal to the cause."

PAT. Haven't you got your initials mixed up? Are you in the I.R.A. or the F.B.I.?

OFFICER. You're an old man, don't take advantage of it.

PAT. I was out in 1916.

OFFICER. And lost your leg, they tell me.

PAT. More than that, You wouldn't recall, I suppose, the time in County Kerry when the agricultural labourers took over five thousand acres of land from Lord Tralee?

OFFICER. No, I would not.

PAT. 1925 it was. They had it all divided fair and square and were ploughing and planting in great style. I.R.A. H.Q. sent down orders that they were to get off the land. That social question would be settled when we'd won the thirty-two-county republic.

OFFICER. Quite right, too.

PAT. The Kerry men said they weren't greedy, they didn't want the whole thirty-two counties, their own five thousand acres would do 'em for a start.

OFFICER. Those men were wrong on the social question.

PAT. It wasn't the question they were interested in, but the answers. Anyway, I agreed with them. I stayed there and trained a unit. By the time I'd finished we could take on the I.R.A., the Free State Army, or the British bloody Navy, if it came to it.

OFFICER. That was mutiny. You should have been court-martialled.

PAT. I was. Court-martialled in my absence, sentenced to death in my absence. So I said, right, you can shoot me —in my absence.

OFFICER. I was told to come here. They must have known what I was coming to. You can understand their reasons for choosing it, the police would never believe we'd use this place. At least you can't be an informer.

PAT. You're a shocking decent person. Could you give me a testimonial in case I wanted to get a job on the Corporation?

OFFICER. I was sent here to arrange certain business. I intend to conclude that business.

PAT. Very well, let us proceed, shall we? When may we expect the prisoner?

OFFICER. Tonight.

PAT. What time?

OFFICER. Between nine and twelve.

PAT. Where is he now?

OFFICER. We haven't got him yet.

PAT. Are you going to Woolworth's to buy one?

OFFICER. I have no business telling you more than has already been communicated to you. The arrangements are made for his reception.

PAT. All except the five pounds for the rent.

OFFICER. I told you I haven't got it.

PAT. Then you'd better get it before your man arrives, or I'll throw the lot of you, prisoner and escort, out—*shun*!

OFFICER. I wouldn't be too sure about that if I were you.
   MEG *and* TERESA *come in.*

MEG. Can we come in now Pat?

PAT. What do you want?

MEG. We want to put the sheets on the bed.

   *There is a blurt of mechanical sound and a commotion upstairs. Everyone in the house rushes in to listen to a portable radio that* COLETTE *is carrying.*

RIO RITA. Mr. Pat, Mr. Pat!

PAT. What is it?

RIO RITA. It's about the boy in the Belfast Jail. They've refused a reprieve.

MULLEADY. The Lord Lieutenant said tomorrow morning, eight o'clock. No reprieve final.

ROPEEN. The boy—the boy in the Belfast Jail?

MULLEADY. Yes—made on behalf of the Government of Northern Ireland.

COLETTE. I've lost it now.

*The radio blurts out music.*

PAT. Turn the bloody thing off.

*Silence.*

MEG. God help us all.

TERESA. The poor boy.

ROPEEN. Eight o'clock in the morning, think of it.

MEG. Ah sure, they might have mercy on him yet. Eighteen years of age—

OFFICER. Irishmen have been hanged by Englishmen at eighteen years of age before now.

PAT. Yes, and Cypriots, Jews and Africans.

MEG. Did you read about them black fellers? Perhaps Mr. de Valera could do something about it.

PAT      ⎫ [*together for once, and with great contempt*].
OFFICER ⎭    Mr. de Valera!

MEG. I'm sure he could stop it if he wanted to. They say he's a very clever man. They say he can speak seven languages.

PAT. It's a terrible pity that English or Irish are not among them, so we'd know what he was saying at odd times.

RIO RITA. Quiet everybody, something's coming through.
COLETTE *repeats the news item from the radio and is echoed by* MULLEADY, ROPEEN, RIO RITA, *and* TERESA:

"Early today a young British soldier was captured as he was coming out of a dance hall in Armagh by the I.R.A. He was put into the back of a car and when last seen was speeding towards the border. All troops have been alerted . . ."

OFFICER. Turn it off, Patrick, get these people out of here.

PAT. I can't do that without making a show of ourselves.

OFFICER. Then come outside with me.

    PAT, I.R.A. OFFICER *and* VOLUNTEER *go out.*

RIO RITA. Who is that man, anyway?

MEG. He's just come about the rent. He's an I.R.A. Officer.

MULLEADY. That poor boy waiting all night for the screws coming for him in the morning.

MEG. Shut up will you?

MULLEADY. I know just how he feels.

MEG. How do you know?

MULLEADY. Well, I was in prison myself once.

MEG. Oh, yes, he was. I forgot.

RIO RITA. Mountjoy?

MULLEADY. As a matter of fact, it was.

RIO RITA. So was I—I'll get you a drink.
    *They all sit at* MULLEADY'S *feet.*

MULLEADY. I was in a cell next to a condemned man.

RIO RITA. What were you in for?

MULLEADY. It was the *Pall Mall Gazette* in 1919.

COLETTE. The what?

MULLEADY. The *Pall Mall Gazette.*

COLETTE. What's that?

MULLEADY. A magazine. There was an advertisement in it for an insurance company and I put all my savings into it. And in return I was to receive an annuity of twenty pounds a year.

MEG. Well, that's not such a vast sum.

ROPEEN. It was in those days.

MULLEADY. Yes, that's the point. When the annuity was due the value of money had declined, so I ran off with the church funds.

MEG. That was a filthy thing to do.

MULLEADY. They put me into prison for that.

RIO RITA. What about the boy in the condemned cell? What had he done?

MULLEADY. Yes, now this is interesting. Flynn, I think his name was. He disposed of his wife and a chicken down a well. Said it was an accident. Said his wife fell down the well trying to retrieve the chicken, but, unfortunately, the police found the wife under the chicken.

COLETTE. How long were you in for?

MULLEADY. Three years.

RIO RITA. You don't look it, dear.

MULLEADY. All this time my younger brother was travelling all over the world.

RIO RITA. They do—don't they?

MULLEADY. Visited every capital in Europe, saw Cardiff, Liverpool, Middlesbrough, went to London—saw Marie Lloyd every night, at the Tivoli.

ROPEEN. Marie Lloyd! She was lovely.

MULLEADY. She may have been, but all that time I was in prison. It broke my poor mother's heart.

MEG. Well, I never caused my poor mother any sorrow, for I never knew her.

MULLEADY. You never had a mother. How very sad.

MEG. I never heard of any living person that didn't have a mother, though I know plenty that don't have fathers. I had one, but I never saw her.

ALL. How sad—I never knew my mother—never to know your mother.

MEG. Are you lot going to sit there all night moaning about your mothers? Did you sweep out your room?

MULLEADY. Well, no.

MEG. Well, go out and get us twelve of stout.
> MULLEADY *goes and talks with* KATE, *the pianist.*
We've run dry by the look of it. And if you're going to sit there you can give us a hand with the beds.

COLETTE. Do you mind—I've been flat on my back all day.

MULLEADY. Kate says the credit has run out.

MEG. Oh Kate, I've got a terrible drought on me.

RIO RITA. I'll tell you what I'll do—I'll run down to the docks and see if I can pick up a sailor—and I'll bring back a crate of Guinness. [*Exit.*]

MEG. Bring the beer back here.

ROPEEN. And the sailor.

> ROPEEN, MULLEADY *and* COLETTE *go,* TERESA *and* MEG *start to make the bed.*

TERESA. There's some very strange people in this house.

MEG. There's some very strange people in the world.

TERESA. I like that big feller. There was no one like him in the convent.

MEG. Do you mean Rio Rita?

TERESA. Yes, it's a gas name, isn't it?

MEG. How long have you been out of the convent?

TERESA. I've just had the one job with the family in Drum-condra.

MEG. Why did you leave there? Did you half-inch some-thing?

TERESA. What did you say?

MEG. Did you half-inch something?

TERESA. I never stole anything in my whole life.

MEG. There's no need to get so upset about it. I never stole anything either. The grand chances I had, too! God doesn't give us these chances twice in a lifetime.

TERESA. It wasn't that; you see, there was a clerical student in the house.

MEG. Well, as far as that's concerned, you'll be a lot safer here. Do the nuns know you left that job in Drumcondra?

TERESA. Oh, no, and they wouldn't be a bit pleased.

MEG. Well, don't say anything to Pat about it. It doesn't do to tell men everything. Here he comes now—don't forget.

PAT *and* MONSEWER *enter from opposite sides along the passage-way.*

Oh, isn't it terrible, Pat? About that poor young man. There's to be no reprieve. Wouldn't it break your heart to be thinking about it?

MONSEWER. It doesn't break my heart.

PAT [*softly*]. It's not your neck they're breaking either.

MONSEWER. It doesn't make me unhappy. It makes me proud; proud to know that the old cause is not dead yet, and that there are still young men willing and ready to go out and die for Ireland.

PAT. I'd say that young man will be in the presence of the Irish martyrs of eight hundred years ago just after eight o'clock tomorrow morning.

MONSEWER. He will. He will. With God's help, he'll be in the company of the heroes.

PAT. My life on yer!

MONSEWER. I would give anything to stand in that young man's place tomorrow morning. For Ireland's sake I would hang crucified in the town square.

PAT. Let's hope it would be a fine day for you.

MONSEWER. I think he's very lucky.

PAT. Very lucky—it's a great pity he didn't buy a sweepstake ticket. [*Coming to* MONSEWER.] You were always a straight man, General, if I may call you by your Christian name. Well, everything is ready for the guest.

MONSEWER. Good. [*Exit.*]

>   Exit PAT *slowly, singing to himself the third verse of "The Laughing Boy" —"Oh, had he died by Pearse's side, or in the G.P.O."*

TERESA. Wasn't that ridiculous talk that old one had out of him?

MEG. Well, Monsewer doesn't look at it like an ordinary person. Monsewer is very given to Ireland and to things of that sort.

TERESA. I think he's an old idiot.

MEG. Monsewer an old idiot? I'll have you know he went to all the biggest colleges in England.

TERESA. It's all the same where he went. He is mad to say

that the death of a young man will make him happy.

MEG. Well, the boy himself said when they sentenced him to death that he was proud and happy to die for Ireland.

TERESA. Ah, but sure, Meg, he hasn't lived yet.

MEG. Have you?

TERESA. A girl of eighteen knows more than a boy of eighteen.

MEG. You could easy do that. That poor young man, he gave no love to any, except to Ireland, and instead of breaking his heart for a girl, it was about the Cause he was breaking it.

TERESA. Well, his white young neck will be broken to-morrow morning anyway.

MEG. Well it's no use mourning him before his time. Come on Kate, give us a bit of music; let's cheer ourselves up.

> *The pianist plays a reel and* MEG *and* TERESA *dance. Gradually everyone else in the house hears the music and comes to join in, until everyone is caught up in a swirling interweaving dance. Through this dance the* SOLDIER *is pushed by the two* I.R.A. *men. He is blind-folded. The dancing falters and the music peters out as the blindfold is whipped from his eyes.*

SOLDIER. Don't stop. I like dancing.

OFFICER. Keep your mouth shut, and get up there.

> *The* SOLDIER *walks slowly up into the room, then turns and sings.*

SOLDIER.         There's no place on earth like the world,
                 There's no place wherever you be.

ALL.             There's no place on earth like the world,
                 That's straight up and take it from me.

| | |
|---|---|
| WOMEN. | Never throw stones at your mother, <br> You'll be sorry for it when she's dead. |
| MEN. | Never throw stones at your mother, <br> Throw bricks at your father instead. |
| MONSEWER. | The South and the north poles are parted, |
| MEG. | Perhaps it is all for the best. |
| PAT. | Till the H-bomb will bring them together, |
| ALL. | And there we will let matters rest. |

CURTAIN

# Act Two

*Later in the same day. The* SOLDIER *is confined in the room. The passage is dark and the lights in the rest of the house are low. The* I.R.A. OFFICER *and the* VOLUNTEER *march along the passage on alternating beats, peering out into the darkness and waiting for a surprise attack that they fear may come. The* VOLUNTEER *carries an old rifle.*

*The house appears to be still, but in the dark corners and doorways, behind the piano and under the stairs, people are hiding, waiting for an opportunity to contact the prisoner, to see what he looks like and to take him comforts like cups of tea, Bible tracts, cigarettes and stout. As soon as the* OFFICER *and the* VOLUNTEER *turn their backs, a scurry of movement is seen and hisses and low whistles are heard. When the* I.R.A. *men turn to look there is silence and stillness. The* I.R.A. *men are growing more and more nervous.*

SOLDIER [*as the* VOLUNTEER *passes him on his sentry beat*].
Psst!

> *The* VOLUNTEER *ignores him, marks time and marches off fast. He re-enters cautiously and marches along his beat.*

Psst!

> *The* VOLUNTEER *peers into the darkness and turns to go.*
Halt!

*The* VOLUNTEER *drops his rifle in fright, recovers it and threatens the* SOLDIER *as the* OFFICER *comes dashing in. In the corners there is a faint scuttling as people hide away.*

OFFICER. What's going on here?

SOLDIER. Any chance of a cigarette?

OFFICER. I don't smoke.

SOLDIER. How about you?

VOLUNTEER. I don't indulge meself. [*He waits until the* OFFICER *has left.*] Ey, you'll get a cup of tea in a minute. [*He marches off.*]

SOLDIER. Smashing. "I'll get a nice cuppa tea in the morning, A nice cuppa tea . . ."

OFFICER. [*rushing back*]. What's the matter now?

SOLDIER. Nothing. [*The* VOLUNTEER *reappears.*]

OFFICER. What's all the noise about?

SOLDIER. I just wondered if she might be bringing my tea.

OFFICER. Who's she?

SOLDIER. You know, the red-headed one—the one we saw first. Bit of all right.

OFFICER. Guard, keep him covered. I'll go and see about his tea.

*The* OFFICER *goes to see about the prisoner's tea. The* VOLUNTEER *resumes his beat. As he turns to go, all hell breaks loose and everyone tries to get to the* SOLDIER *at once. People hare through the room at breakneck speed, leaving the* SOLDIER *with stout, hymn sheets, aspidistras, and words of comfort.*

COLETTE. Five minutes—upstairs—I won't charge you.

*The* VOLUNTEER *attempts to stop them all at once and only gets more and more confused until* PAT *enters and drives everyone offstage. The lines of this scene are largely improvised to suit the situation.*

PAT. Come on, out of here, you lot. Get out, will you!

ROPEEN. I'm only going to the piano.

*They all go and* PAT *calls* TERESA. PAT *and the* VOLUNTEER *leave as* TERESA *comes downstairs with the* SOLDIER'S *tea on a tray. She goes to leave straight away, but he stops her.*

SOLDIER. Ey! I liked your dancing . . . you know, the old-knees-up . . . Is that mine?

TERESA. Yes, it's your tea— sure you must be starving. Your belly must be stuck to your back with hunger.

SOLDIER. A bit of all right, isn't it?

TERESA. You're lucky. Meg gave you two rashers.

SOLDIER. Did she now?

TERESA. She said you must have double the meal of a grown person.

SOLDIER. Why's that?

TERESA. Because you have two jobs to do.

SOLDIER. What are they?

TERESA. To grow up big and strong like all lads.

SOLDIER. Here, I'm older than you, I bet.

TERESA. I think you look like a young lad.

SOLDIER. You look like a kid yourself. How old are you?

TERESA. I'm nineteen.

SOLDIER. Are you? I'm nineteen, too. When's your date of birth?

TERESA. January. Twenty-fifth of January. When were you born?

SOLDIER. August. [*He is shamed.*]

TERESA. So you see, I'm older than you.

SOLDIER. Only a few weeks.

TERESA. What name do we call you?

SOLDIER. Leslie. What's yours?

TERESA. Teresa.

SOLDIER. Teresa. That's proper Irish, ain't it?

TERESA. Well, it is Irish.

SOLDIER. Yeah, that's what I said. Teresa, you haven't got a fag have you?

TERESA. A what?

SOLDIER. A fag. [*He makes a gesture with his fingers for a fag which* TERESA *thinks is an invitation to bed.*] Smoke— cigarette.

TERESA. No, thank you. I don't smoke.

SOLDIER. No, not for you—for me.

TERESA. Oh, for you. Wait a minute. Look, it's only a bit crushed. Pat gave it to me. [*She gives him a crumpled cigarette.*]

SOLDIER. Have you got a match—they took mine.

TERESA *gives him matches.*

Hey, don't go. I suppose you couldn't get me a packet?

TERESA. I'll get you twenty Afton.

SOLDIER. Oh no. I mean—thanks, anyway. Ten'll do.

TERESA. You don't fancy the Irish cigarettes?

SOLDIER. What? The old Aftons? I love 'em. Smoke 'em by the barrer-load.

TERESA. I'll get you twenty. You've a long night ahead of you.

> TERESA *gets money from* KATE, *the pianist, who is standing offstage. The* SOLDIER, *left completely alone for the first time, has a quick run round the room, looking through doors and windows. He lifts the clothes and looks under the bed.* TERESA *returns.*

TERESA. Are you looking for something.?

SOLDIER. No. Yes, an ashtray.

TERESA. Under the bed?

SOLDIER. Well, I might have been looking for the in and the out, mightn't I?

TERESA. What?

SOLDIER. The way out. I'm a prisoner, ain't I?

TERESA. I'd better go.

SOLDIER. You'll be back with the fags?

TERESA. I might. I only work here, you know.

> TERESA *goes and the* SOLDIER *moves to all the doors in turn and calls out:*

SOLDIER. Hey! Charlie! Buffalo Bill!

> *The* VOLUNTEER *rushes on, thinking an attack has started, does not see the* SOLDIER *in the corner of the room and prepares to defend the front. The* SOLDIER *calls him back and whispers to him.* PAT *comes downstairs.*

PAT. What's he saying?

VOLUNTEER. He wants to go round the back, sir.

PAT. Well, he can, can't he?

VOLUNTEER. No, sir. I'm in the same plight myself, but I can't leave me post for two hours yet.

PAT. Why don't you both go?

VOLUNTEER. We'll have to ask the officer.

PAT. Well, I'll call him. Sir, St. Patrick. Sir.

> *The* OFFICER *enters in a panic.*

OFFICER. What the hell's going on here?

PAT. It's your man here . . .

> *The* OFFICER *silences him and leads him out into the passage.* PAT *whispers in his ear. The* OFFICER *comes to attention.*

[*To the audience.*] A man wants to go round the back and it's a military secret.

OFFICER. Right. Prisoner and escort, fall in. [PAT *and the* VOLUNTEER *fall in on either side of the* SOLDIER.] Prisoner and escort, right turn. By the front, quick march . . . left . . . right. [*They march right round the room to the lavatory door.*] HALT! Prisoner, fall out. You two guard the door. [TERESA *rushes into the room with the twenty Afton, sees the* OFFICER *and starts to rush out again, but he spots her.*] You girl, come back here. What are you doing here?

TERESA. I was just going to give him his cigarettes, sir.

OFFICER. What is this man to you?

TERESA. Nothing, sir.

OFFICER. Give them to me.

TERESA. But they're his.

OFFICER. Give them to me.

> *She gives him the cigarettes. The parade returns.*

PAT. Fall in. Quick march—left right, etc. Halt. One man relieved, sir.

VOLUNTEER. What about me?

OFFICER. Silence.

TERESA. Where has he been?

PAT. Doing a job that no one else could do for him.

TERESA. Leslie, I got you . . .

OFFICER. That's enough. Get along with you, girl. About your business.

*Exit* TERESA. *The* I.R.A. OFFICER *watches her go.*

Patrick, is that girl all right?

PAT. Oh, come on, sir. You don't want to be thinking about that, and you on duty, too.

OFFICER. I mean will she keep her mouth shut?

PAT. Sure now, you know what women are like. They're always talking about these things—did you have a bit last night? But I don't think she'd fancy you somehow.

OFFICER. I'm asking you if she's to be trusted.

PAT. You mean would she help your man to escape?

OFFICER. Now you have it.

PAT. She'd do nothing to bring the police here. And as for helping him get away, she's all for keeping him here. They're getting along very well, those two.

OFFICER. Yes, a bit too well for my liking.

PAT. Well, she's passing the time for him. Better than having him fighting and all. Sure, they're getting along like a couple of budgeriguards.

OFFICER. This is no laughing matter, you idiot.

PAT. You know, there are two kinds of gunmen. The earnest, religious-minded ones like you, and the laughing boys.

OFFICER. Like you.

PAT. Well, you know, in the time of the troubles it was always the laughing boys who were most handy with the skit.

OFFICER. Why?

PAT. Because it's not a natural thing for a man with a sense of humour to be tricking with firearms and fighting. There must be something wrong with him.

OFFICER. There must be something the matter with you, then.

PAT. Of course there is. Ey, what about the money for the rent?

OFFICER. At this moment the hearts of all true Irishmen are beating for us, fighting as we are to save the Belfast martyr, and all you can think about is money.

PAT. Well, you see, I'm not a hero. I'm what you might call an ex-hero. And if we get raided . . .

OFFICER. I refuse to envisage such a possibility.

PAT. All the same, if we are raided. You can say I only did it for the money.

OFFICER. We shall fight to the death.

PAT. You're all in the running for a hero's death.

OFFICER. I hope I would never betray my trust.

PAT. You've never been in prison for the cause.

OFFICER. No. I have not.

PAT. That's easily seen.

OFFICER. You have, of course.

PAT. Nine years, in all.

OFFICER. Nine years in English prisons?

PAT. Irish prisons part of the time.

OFFICER. The loss of liberty is a terrible thing.

PAT. That's not the worst thing, nor the redcaps, nor the screws. Do you know what the worst thing is?

OFFICER. No.

PAT. The other Irish patriots in along with you.

OFFICER. What did you say?

PAT. Your fellow patriots, in along with you. There'd be a split straight away.

OFFICER. If I didn't know you were out in 1916 . . .

*Bagpipes have been playing in the distance and the sound comes steadily nearer. Everyone in the house crowds down into the passage area and stares out front as though they are looking through two windows, straining to get a sight of the procession in the street.*

MEG. Teresa—Teresa—it's a band!

PAT. What's going on?

MEG. They're marching to the G.P.O. over the boy that's being hung in the Belfast Jail.

PAT. It's like Jim Larkin's funeral.

VOLUNTEER. Plenty of police about.

MONSEWER. By Jove, look at those banners. "Another victim for occupied Ireland."

MEG. "England, the hangman of thousands. In Ireland, in Kenya, in Cyprus."

MULLEADY. "Release the Belfast martyr!"

MEG. The world will see a day when England will be that low you won't be able to walk on her.

RIO RITA. "Eighteen years of age, in jail for Ireland."

ROPEEN. ⎫
COLETTE. ⎰ Ah, the poor boy.

MEG. Oh, the murdering bastards.

> *The* SOLDIER *comes down to the front of the stage and tries to explain to the audience what is happening.*

SOLDIER. You know what they're on about, don't you? This bloke in the Belfast Jail who's going to be topped tomorrow morning. You read about it, didn't you? Papers were full of it over here—headlines that big. He's only eighteen, same age as us National Service blokes. Anyway, they got him, and tomorrow they're going to do him in—eight o'clock in the morning.

> *The pipes fade away and the groups break up.*

MEG. That's the end of it.

PAT. Thanks be to God we don't all go that way.

MONSEWER. It was a good turn-out, Patrick. [*He leaves.*]

PAT. It was, sir.

MISS GILCHRIST. I shan't sleep a wink all night.

RIO RITA. Ah you murdering bastard. Why don't you go back home to your own country?

SOLDIER. You can take me out of it as soon as you like. I never bloody-well asked to be brought here.

> *The first person to take advantage of the* I.R.A. OFFICER'S *absence and the* VOLUNTEER'S *confusion is* MISS GILCHRIST. *While the* VOLUNTEER *is striving to keep* MULLEADY *and* COLETTE *out of the room,* MISS GILCHRIST *slips behind his back, the* VOLUNTEER *turns, and soon* MULLEADY, COLETTE *and* ROPEEN *are inside the room with* MISS GILCHRIST. *They crowd round the* SOLDIER *and paw and stroke him.*

MISS GILCHRIST. Is this the English boy? May I give him a little gift?

PAT. What is it?

MISS GILCHRIST. It's an article from a newspaper and as it's about his own dear Queen, I thought it might comfort him.

PAT. Come here.

MISS GILCHRIST. No, Mr. Pat, I insist. [*She reads from a paper*.][1] It's from the *Daily Express* and it's called "Within the Palace Walls". "Within the Palace Walls. So much is known of the Queen's life on the surface, so little about how her life is really run. But now this article has been written with the active help of the Queen's closest advisers."

SOLDIER. No, thank you, ma'am, I don't go in for that sort of mullarkey. Haven't you got something else?

MULLEADY. Evangelina!

MISS GILCHRIST. Who calls?

MULLEADY. Me! Me! Me! Me! Bookie, please! Please!

MISS GILCHRIST. Well, if the boy doesn't want it . . .

SOLDIER. Quite sure, thank you, ma'am.

MULLEADY. May I read on, please?

MISS GILCHRIST. Go on, Eustace.

MULLEADY [*savouring and drooling over each phrase*]. "Because it is completely fresh, probing hitherto un-reported aspects of her problems, this intriguing new serial lays before you the true pattern of the Queen's life with understanding, intimacy and detail." Oh may I keep it, Miss Gilchrist?

[1]This extract was varied to keep it as topical as possible within the context of the scene.

PAT. Give it here. [*He snatches the paper from* MULLEADY.] We don't go in for that sort of nonsense. [*He looks at the article.*] Would you believe it. It's by an Irishman. Dermot Morrah!

RIO RITA. I don't believe it.

MEG. Never! And she calls herself an Irishwoman, the silly bitch.

> *The Irish patriots leave the stage. Those remaining in the room are pro-English, sentimental, or both.* MISS GILCHRIST *comes down to address the audience.*[1]

MISS GILCHRIST. I have nothing against the Royal Family. I think they're all lovely, especially that Sister Rowe and Uffa Fox. I get all the Sunday Papers to follow them up. One paper contradicts another, but you put two and two together—and you might almost be in the yacht there with them. And there's that Mrs. Dale, she's a desperate nice woman. I always send her a bunch of flowers on her birthday. They even have an Irishman in it, a Mr. O'Malley. He keeps a hotel, like you, Mr. Pat. [PAT *has gone long ago.*]

MULLEADY [*picking up the paper from where* PAT *threw it*]. I'll get this paper every day. It will be my Bible.

SOLDIER. Well, personally mate, I'd sooner have the Bible. I read it once on jankers.

MISS GILCHRIST. Is this true?

SOLDIER. It's blue, ma'am.

MISS GILCHRIST [*enraptured*]. My favourite colour.

---

[1]Uffa Fox and Sister Rowe were two examples of people whose names were so closely linked with royalty that the distinction became blurred. Other names used were Armstrong-Jones before his marriage, several Maharajahs and Billy Wallace.

SOLDIER. You'd like it then, ma'am. All you've got to do
is sort out the blue bits from the dreary bits and you're
laughing.

MISS GILCHRIST. May we sing to you?

SOLDIER. If you like.

> MISS GILCHRIST *and* MULLEADY *assemble themselves on
> either side of the table and pose.* ROPEEN *places an
> aspidistra in the centre of the table. They sing to the
> tune of "Danny Boy".*

MISS GILCHRIST.

You read the Bible, in its golden pages,
You read those words and talking much of love.
You read the works of Plato and the sages,
They tell of hope, and joy, and peace and love.

MULLEADY.

But I'm afraid it's all a lot of nonsense,
About as true as leprechaun or elf.

BOTH.

You realize, when you want somebody,
That there is no one, no one, loves you like yourself.

MULLEADY.

I did my best to be a decent person,
I drove a tram for Murphy in thirteen.
I failed to pass my medical for the Army,
But loyally tried to serve my King and Queen.
Through all the troubled times I was no traitor,
Even when the British smashed poor mother's Delft.
And when they left, I became a loyal Free-Stater.
But, I know there is no one, no one loves you like your-
self.

MULLEADY WITH MISS GILCHRIST [*Crooning in harmony*].

I really think us lower-middle classes,
Get thrown around just like snuff at a wake.
Employers take us for a set of asses,
The rough, they sneer at all attempts we make
To have nice manners and to speak correctly,
And in the end we're flung upon the shelf.
We have no unions, cost of living bonus,

BOTH.

It's plain to see that no one, no one loves you like yourself.

> PAT *catches them singing and drives everyone off the stage except the* SOLDIER.

PAT. Come on, get out, will you? [*To the* SOLDIER.] Never mind that old idiot, if you want to go round the back again, just give me a shout.

SOLDIER. What if you're asleep?

PAT. I haven't slept a wink since 8th May 1921.

SOLDIER. Did you have an accident?

PAT. I had three. I was bashed, booted and bayoneted in Arbourhill Barracks.

SOLDIER. Redcaps. Bastards, aren't they?

PAT. They are, each and every one.

> PAT *goes off.*

TERESA [*entering*]. Leslie, Leslie, hey, Leslie.

SOLDIER. Hello, Ginger—come into me castle.

TERESA. Did you get your cigarettes?

SOLDIER. No.

TERESA. Did the officer not give them to you?

SOLDIER. No.

TERESA *swears in Irish.*

'Ere, 'ere, 'ere, you mustn't swear. Anyway, you should never trust officers.

TERESA. Well, I got you a few anyway.

*There is a mournful blast off from* MONSEWER'S *pipes.*

SOLDIER. What's that?

TERESA. It's Monsewer practising his pipes.

SOLDIER. He's what?

TERESA. He's practising his pipes. He's going to play a lament.

SOLDIER. A lament?

TERESA. For the boy in Belfast Jail.

SOLDIER. You mean a dirge. He's going to need a lot of practice.

TERESA. Don't make a jeer about it. [*The bagpipes stop.*]

SOLDIER. I'm not jeering. I feel sorry for the poor bloke, but that noise won't help him, will it?

TERESA. Well, he's one of your noble lot, anyway.

SOLDIER. What do you mean, he's one of our noble lot?

TERESA. Monsewer is—he went to college with your king.

SOLDIER. We ain't got one.

TERESA. Maybe he's dead now, but you had one one time, didn't you?

SOLDIER. We got a duke now. He plays tiddlywinks.

TERESA. Anyway, he left your lot and came over here and fought for Ireland.

SOLDIER. Why, was somebody doing something to Ireland?

TERESA. Wasn't England, for hundreds of years?

SOLDIER. That was donkey's years ago. Everybody was doing something to someone in those days.

TERESA. And what about today? What about the boy in Belfast Jail? Do you know that in the six counties the police walk the beats in tanks and armoured cars.

SOLDIER. If he was an Englishman they'd hang him just the same.

TERESA. It's because of the English being in Ireland that he fought.

SOLDIER. And what about the Irish in London? Thousands of them. Nobody's doing anything to them. We just let them drink their way through it. That's London for you. That's where we should be, down the 'dilly on a Saturday night.

TERESA. You're as bad as the Dublin people here.

SOLDIER. You're one of them, aren't you?

TERESA. I'm no Dubliner.

SOLDIER. What are you—a country yokel?

TERESA. I was reared in the convent at Ballymahon.

SOLDIER. I was reared down the Old Kent Road.

TERESA. Is that where your father and mother live?

SOLDIER. I ain't got none.

TERESA. You're not an orphan, are you?

SOLDIER. Yes, I'm one of the little orphans of the storm.

TERESA. You're a terrible chancer.

SOLDIER. Well, actually, my old lady ran off with a Pole, not that you'd blame her if you knew my old man.

*The bagpipes are heard again, louder and nearer.*

TERESA. He's coming in.

> MONSEWER *and* PAT *enter from opposite sides of the stage and slow march towards each other.*

SOLDIER. Cor, look at that, skirt and all.

> MONSEWER *stops to adjust the pipes and continues.*

You know the only good thing about them pipes? They don't smell.

> PAT *and* MONSEWER *meet and halt. The bagpipes fade with a sad belch.*

MONSEWER. Not so good, eh, Patrick?

PAT. No, sir.

MONSEWER. Never mind, we'll get there.

PAT. Yes, sir.

MONSEWER [*gives* PAT *the pipes*]. Weekly troop inspection, Patrick.

PATRICK. Oh, yes, sir. [*Shouts.*] Come on, fall in. Come on, all you Gaels and Republicans on the run, get fell in.

> *Everyone in the house, except* MEG *and the* I.R.A. OFFICER, *rushes on and lines up.*

SOLDIER. Me an' all?

PAT. Yes, get on the end. Right dress. [*The "troops" stamp their feet and someone shouts "Olé".*] Attention. All present and correct sir.

MONSEWER. Fine body of men. [*He walks down the line inspecting. To* PRINCESS GRACE.] Colonials, eh? [*To* RIO RITA.] Keep the powder dry, laddie.

RIO RITA. I'll try, sir.

MONSEWER [*to* COLETTE]. You're doing a great job, my dear.

COLETTE. Thank you, sir.

E

MONSEWER [*to the* VOLUNTEER]. Name?

VOLUNTEER. O'Connor, sir.

MONSEWER. Station?

VOLUNTEER. Irish State Railways, Central Station, No. 3 platform.

MONSEWER [*to the* SOLDIER]. Name?

SOLDIER. Williams, sir, Leslie A.

MONSEWER.  Station?

SOLDIER. Armagh, sir.

MONSEWER. Like it?

SOLDIER. No, sir, it's a dump, sir. [*To* PAT.] It is, you know, mate, shocking. Everything closes down at ten. You can't get a drink on a Sunday.

*The parade dissolves into a shambles.*

PAT. Can't get a drink?

SOLDIER. No.

MONSEWER. Patrick, is this the English laddie?

PAT. Yes, sir.

MONSEWER. Good God! We've made a bloomer. Dismiss the troops.

PAT. Troops, dismiss. Come on, there's been a mistake. Get off.

*They go, except* TERESA.

SOLDIER [*to* PAT]. She don't have to go, does she?

PAT. No, she's all right.

MONSEWER. What's that girl doing, fraternizing?

PAT. Not at the moment, sir. She's just remaking the bed.

MONSEWER. I'm going to question the prisoner, Patrick.

PAT. Yes, sir.

MONSEWER. Strictly according to the rules laid down by the Geneva Convention.

PAT. Oh yes, sir.

MONSEWER [*to the* SOLDIER]. Name?

SOLDIER. Williams, sir. Leslie A.

MONSEWER. Rank?

SOLDIER. Private.

MONSEWER. Number?

SOLDIER. 23774486.

MONSEWER. That's the lot, carry on.

SOLDIER. Can I ask you a question, guv?

MONSEWER. Can he, Patrick?

PAT. Permission to ask a question, sir. One step forward, march.

SOLDIER. What are those pipes actually for?

MONSEWER. Those pipes, my boy, are the instrument of the ancient Irish race.

SOLDIER. Permission to ask another question, sir.

PAT. One step forward, march.

SOLDIER. What actually is a race, guv?

MONSEWER. A race occurs when a lot of people live in one place for a long period of time.

SOLDIER. I reckon our old sergeant-major must be a race; he's been stuck in that same depot for about forty years.

MONSEWER [*in Irish*]. Focail, Focaileile uait.

SOLDIER. Smashing-looking old geezer, ain't he? Just like our old Colonel back at the depot. Same face, same voice. Gorblimey, I reckon it is him.

MONSEWER. Sleachta—sleachta.

SOLDIER. Is he a free Hungarian, or something?

MONSEWER. Sleachta—sleachta.

SOLDIER. Oh. That's Garlic, ain't it?

MONSEWER. That, my dear young man, is Gaelic. A language old before the days of the Greeks.

SOLDIER. Did he say Greeks?

PAT. Yes, Greeks.

SOLDIER. Excuse me, guv. I can't have you running down the Greeks. Mate of mine's a Greek, runs a caffee down the Edgware Road. Best Rosy Lee and Holy Ghost in London.

MONSEWER. Rosy Lee and Holy Ghost . . . ? What abomination is this?

SOLDIER. C. of E., guv.

PAT. Cockney humour, sir.

MONSEWER. The language of Shakespeare and Milton.

SOLDIER. He can't make up his mind, can he?

MONSEWER. That's the trouble with the fighting forces today. No background, no tradition, no morale.

SOLDIER. We got background—we got tradition. They gave us all that at the Boys' Home. They gave us team spirit, fair play, cricket.

MONSEWER. Are you a cricketer, my boy?

SOLDIER. Yes, sir. Do you like a game?

MONSEWER. By Jove, yes.

SOLDIER. Mind you, I couldn't get on with it at the Boys' Home. They gave us two sets of stumps, you see, and I'd always been used to one, chalked up on the old wall at home.

MONSEWER. That's not cricket, my boy.

SOLDIER. Now there you are, then. You're what I call a cricket person and I'm what I call a soccer person. That's where your race lark comes in.

MONSEWER. Ah, cricket. By Jove, that takes me back. Strange how this uncouth youth has brought back memories of summers long past. Fetch the pianist, Patrick. A little light refreshment. [ROPEEN *brings him tea.*] Thank you, my dear, two lumps.

*As he sings of summers long forgotten, the genteel people of the house sip tea and listen—*MULLEADY, MISS GILCHRIST *and* ROPEEN.

*He sings:*

> I remember in September,
> When the final stumps were drawn,
> And the shouts of crowds now silent
> And the boys to tea were gone.
> Let us, oh Lord above us,
> Still remember simple things,
> When all are dead who love us,
> Oh the Captains and the Kings,
> When all are dead who love us,
> Oh the Captains and the Kings.
>
> We have many goods for export,
> Christian ethics and old port,
> But our greatest boast is that
> The Anglo-Saxon is a sport.
> On the playing-fields of Eton
> We still do thrilling things,
> Do not think we'll ever weaken
> Up the Captains and the Kings!
> Do not think we'll ever weaken
> Up the Captains and the Kings!

Far away in dear old Cyprus,
Or in Kenya's dusty land,
Where all bear the white man's burden
In many a strange land.
As we look across our shoulder
In West Belfast the school bell rings,
And we sigh for dear old England,
And the Captains and the Kings.
And we sigh for dear old England,
And the Captains and the Kings.

In our dreams we see old Harrow,
And we hear the crow's loud caw,
At the flower show our big marrow
Takes the prize from Evelyn Waugh.
Cups of tea or some dry sherry,
Vintage cars, these simple things,
So let's drink up and be merry
Oh, the Captains and the Kings.
So, let's drink up and be merry
Oh, the Captains and the Kings.

I wandered in a nightmare
All around Great Windsor Park,
And what do you think I found there
As I stumbled in the dark?
'Twas an apple half-bitten,
And sweetest of all things,
Five baby teeth had written
Of the Captain and the Kings.
Five baby teeth had written
Of the Captains and the Kings.

By the moon that shines above us
In the misty morn and night,

Let us cease to run ourselves down
But praise God that we are white.
And better still we're English—
Tea and toast and muffin rings,
Old ladies with stern faces,
And the Captains and the Kings.
Old ladies with stern faces,
And the Captains and the Kings.[1]

*A quavering bugle blows a staggering salute offstage.*

PAT. Well, that's brought the show to a standstill.

OFFICER. Patrick, get that old idiot out of here.

*The two* I.R.A. *men have been listening horror-stricken to the last verse of the song.*

Guard!

VOLUNTEER. Sir.

OFFICER. No one is to be allowed in here, do you understand? No one.

VOLUNTEER. I understand, sir. Might I be relieved from my post?

OFFICER. Certainly not. [*The* VOLUNTEER *is bursting.*]

VOLUNTEER. Two minutes, sir.

OFFICER. No, certainly not. Get back to your post. This place is like a rabbit warren with everyone skipping about.

*The* VOLUNTEER *hobbles off.*

MONSEWER. Ah, the laddie from headquarters. There you are.

---

[1]Actually, he never sings all of this song, as there isn't time. The usual order is to sing verses 1, 4, and 6, with one of the other verses optional.

OFFICER. Yes, here I am. You being an old soldier will understand the need for discipline.

MONSEWER. Quite right, too.

OFFICER. I must ask you what you were doing in here.

MONSEWER. Inspecting the prisoner.

OFFICER. I'm afraid I must ask you to keep out of here in future.

MONSEWER. Patrick, I know this young man has been working under a strain, but—there's no need to treat me like an Empire Loyalist. You know where to find me when you need me, Patrick. [*He sweeps off.*]

PAT. Yes, sir.

MONSEWER [*as he goes*]. Chin up, sonny.

SOLDIER. Cheerio, sir.

OFFICER. I've had enough of this nonsense. I'll inspect the prisoner myself. [TERESA *is seen to be under the bed.*]

PAT. Yes, sir. Stand by your bed.

OFFICER. One pace forward, march.

SOLDIER. Can I ask you what you intend to do with me, sir?

OFFICER. You keep your mouth shut and no harm will come to you. Have you got everything you want?

SOLDIER. Oh yes, sir.

OFFICER. Right. Take over, Patrick. I'm going to inspect the outposts.

PAT. Have you got the place well covered, sir?

OFFICER. I have indeed. Why?

PAT. I think it's going to rain.

OFFICER. No more tomfoolery, please.

I.R.A. OFFICER *and* PATRICK *depart, leaving* TERESA *alone with* LESLIE.

SOLDIER. You can come out now.

TERESA. No, he might see me.

SOLDIER. He's gone, he won't be back for a long time. Come on, sit down and tell me a story—the Irish are great at that, aren't they?

TERESA. Well, not all of them. I'm not. I don't know any stories.

SOLDIER. Anything'll do. It doesn't have to be funny. It's just something to pass the time.

TERESA. Yes, you've a long night ahead of you, and so has he.

SOLDIER. Who?

TERESA. You know, the boy in Belfast.

SOLDIER. What do you have to mention him for?

TERESA. I'm sorry, Leslie.

SOLDIER. It's all right, it's just that everybody's been talking about the boy in the Belfast Jail.

TERESA. Will I tell you about when I was a girl in the convent?

SOLDIER. Yeah, that should be a bit of all right. Go on.

TERESA. Oh, it was the same as any other school, except you didn't go home. You played in a big yard which had a stone floor; you'd break your bones if you fell on it. But there was a big meadow outside the wall, we used to be let out there on our holidays. It was lovely. We were brought swimming a few times, too, that was really terrific, but the nuns were terrible strict, and if they saw a man come within a mile of us, well we . . .

SOLDIER. What? . . . Aw, go on, Teresa, we're grown-ups now, aren't we?

TERESA. We were not allowed to take off our clothes at all. You see, Leslie, even when we had our baths on Saturday nights they put shifts on all the girls.

SOLDIER. Put what on yer?

TERESA. A sort of sheet, you know.

SOLDIER. Oh yeah.

TERESA. Even the little ones four of five years of age.

SOLDIER. Oh, we never had anything like that.

TERESA. What did you have?

SOLDIER. Oh no, we never had anything like that. I mean, in our place we had all showers and we were sloshing water over each other—and blokes shouting and screeching and making a row—it was smashing! Best night of the week, it was.

TERESA. Our best time was the procession for the Blessed Virgin.

SOLDIER. Blessed who?

TERESA. Shame on you, the Blessed Virgin. Anyone would think you were a Protestant.

SOLDIER. I am, girl.

TERESA. Oh, I'm sorry.

SOLDIER. That's all right. Never think about it myself.

TERESA. Anyway, we had this big feast.

SOLDIER. Was the scoff good?

TERESA. The—what?

SOLDIER. The grub. The food. You don't understand me half the time, do you?

TERESA. Well, we didn't have food. It was a feast day. We just used to walk around.

SOLDIER. You mean they didn't give you nothing at all? Well, blow that for a lark.

TERESA. Well, are you going to listen to me story? Well, are you? Anyway, we had this procession, and I was looking after the mixed infants.

SOLDIER. What's a mixed infant.

TERESA. A little boy or girl under five years of age. Because up until that time they were mixed together.

SOLDIER. I wish I'd been a mixed infant.

TERESA. Do you want to hear my story? When the boys were six they were sent to the big boys' orphanage.

SOLDIER. You're one, too—an orphan? You didn't tell me that.

TERESA. Yes, I did.

SOLDIER. We're quits now.

TERESA. I didn't believe your story.

SOLDIER. Well, it's true. Anyway, never mind. Tell us about this mixed infant job.

TERESA. There was this little feller, his father was dead, and his mother had run away or something. All the other boys were laughing and shouting, but this one little boy was all on his own and he was crying like the rain. Nothing would stop him. So, do you know what I did, Leslie? I made a crown of daisies and a daisy chain to put round his neck and told him he was King of the May. Do you know he forgot everything except that he was King of the May.

SOLDIER. Would you do that for me if I was a mixed infant?

*They have forgotten all about Belfast Jail and the I.R.A.*
LESLIE *takes* TERESA'S *hand and she moves away. She goes to the window to cover her shyness.*

TERESA. There's a clock striking somewhere in the city.

SOLDIER. I wonder what time it is?

TERESA. I don't know.

SOLDIER. Will you give me a picture of yourself, Teresa?

TERESA. What for?

SOLDIER. Just to have. I mean, they might take me away in the middle of the night and I might never see you again.

TERESA. I'm not Marilyn Monroe or Jayne Mansfield.

SOLDIER. Who wants a picture of them? They're all old.

TERESA. I haven't got one anyway.

*She pulls out a medal which she has round her neck.*

SOLDIER. What's that?

TERESA. It's a medal. It's for you, Leslie.

SOLDIER. I'm doing all right, ain't I? In the army nine months and I get a medal already.

TERESA. It's not that kind of medal.

SOLDIER. Let's have a look . . . looks a bit like you.

TERESA [*shocked*]. No Leslie,.

SOLDIER. Oh, it's that lady of yours.

TERESA. It's God's mother.

SOLDIER. Yes, that one.

TERESA. She's the mother of everyone else in the world, too. Will you wear it round your neck?

SOLDIER. I will if you put it on.

*She puts it over his head and he tries to kiss her.*

TERESA. Leslie. Don't. Why do you have to go and spoil everything—I'm going.

SOLDIER. Don't go! Let's pretend we're on the films, where all I have to say is "Let me", and all you have to say is "Yes".

TERESA. Oh, all right.

SOLDIER. Come on, Kate.

*They sing and dance.*

> I will give you a golden ball,
> To hop with the children in the hall,

TERESA. If you'll marry, marry, marry, marry,
> If you'll marry me.

SOLDIER. I will give you the keys of my chest,
> And all the money that I possess,

TERESA. If you'll marry, marry, marry, marry,
> If you'll marry me.

SOLDIER. I will give you a watch and chain,
> To show the kids in Angel Lane,

TERESA. If you'll marry, marry, marry, marry,
> If you'll marry me.
> I will bake you a big pork pie,
> And hide you till the cops go by,

BOTH. If you'll marry, marry, marry, marry,
> If you'll marry me.

SOLDIER. But first I think that we should see,
> If we fit each other,

TERESA. [*To the audience*]. Shall we?

SOLDIER. Yes, let's see.

*They run to the bed. The lights black out.* MISS GILCHRIST *rushes on and a spotlight comes up on her.*

MISS GILCHRIST [*horrified*]. They're away. [*To* KATE.] My music, please!

> *She sings:* Only a box of matches
>                 I send, dear mother, to thee.
>                 Only a box of matches,
>                 Across the Irish sea.
>                 I met with a Gaelic pawnbroker,
>                 From Killarney's waterfalls,
>                 With sobs he cried, "I wish I had died,
>                 The Saxons have stolen my—

PAT *rushes on to stop her saying "balls" and drags her off, curtsying and singing again*—

> Only a box of matches— —

MEG *enters the darkened passage.*

MEG. Teresa! Teresa!

> *The* VOLUNTEER *enters in hot pursuit.*

VOLUNTEER. Ey, you can't go in there. Sir! Sir!

> *The* OFFICER *enters and blocks* MEG's *passage.*

Sir, there's another woman trying to get in to him.

OFFICER. You can't go in there. Security forbids it.

VOLUNTEER. Common decency forbids it. He might not have his trousers on.

MEG. Auah, do you think I've never seen a man with his trousers off before?

OFFICER. I'd be very much surprised if you'd ever seen one with them on.

MEG. Thanks.

VOLUNTEER. He's a decent boy, for all he's a British soldier.

MEG. Ah, there's many a good heart beats under a khaki tunic.

VOLUNTEER. There's something in that. My own father was in the Royal Irish Rifles.

OFFICER. Mine was in the Inniskillings.

MEG. And mine was the parish priest.

OFFICER [*horrified*]. God forbid you, woman. After saying that, I won't let you in at all.

MEG. I'm not that particular. I was going about my business till he stopped me.

PAT. You might as well let her go in—cheer him up a bit.

OFFICER. I don't think we should. He's in our care and we're morally responsible for his spiritual welfare.

VOLUNTEER. Well, only in a temporal way, sir.

MEG. I only wanted to see him in a temporal way.

OFFICER. Jesus, Mary and Joseph, it would be a terrible thing for him to die with a sin of impurity on his—

*The lights go up.*

SOLDIER [*running downstage from the bed*]. Die, What's all this talk about dying? Who's going to die?

MEG. We're all going to die, but not before Christmas, we hope.

PAT. Now look what you've done. You'll have to her let in now. You should have been more discreet, surely.

OFFICER. Two minutes then.

*The* I.R.A. OFFICER *and the* VOLUNTEER *move away.* TERESA *stands by the bed,* MEG *goes into the room.*

MEG. She's there, she's been there all the time.

TERESA. I was just dusting, Meg.

MEG. What's wrong with a bit of comfort on a dark night? Are you all right, lad?

SOLDIER. Mum, what are they going to do with me?

MEG. I don't know—I only wish I did.

SOLDIER. Will you go and ask them, because I don't think they know themselves.

MEG. Maybe they don't know, maybe a lot of people don't know, or maybe they've forgotten.

SOLDIER. I don't know what you mean.

MEG. There are some things you can't forget.

SOLDIER. Forget?

MEG. Like here in Russell Street, right next to the place where I was born, the British turned a tank and fired shells into people's homes.

SOLDIER. I suppose it was the war, missus.

MEG. Yes, it was war. Do you know who it was against?

SOLDIER. No.

MEG. Old men and women, the bedridden and the cripples, and mothers with their infants.

SOLDIER. Why them?

MEG. Everybody that was able to move had run away. In one room they found an old woman, her son's helmet and gas mask were still hanging on the wall. He had died fighting on the Somme.

SOLDIER. I don't know nothing about it, lady.

MEG. Would you like to hear some more? Then listen.

*A military drum beats, the piano plays softly, and* MEG *chants rather than sings:*

Who fears to speak of Easter Week
That week of famed renown,
When the boys in green went out to fight
The forces of the Crown.

With Mausers bold, and hearts of gold,
The Red Countess dressed in green,
And high above the G.P.O.
The rebel flag was seen.

Then came ten thousand khaki coats,
Our rebel boys to kill,
Before they reached O'Connell Street,
Of fight they got their fill.

*As she sings everyone else in the house comes slowly on to listen to her.*

They had machine-guns and artillery,
And cannon in galore,
But it wasn't our fault that e'er one
Got back to England's shore.

For six long days we held them off,
At odds of ten to one,
And through our lines they could not pass,
For all their heavy guns.

And deadly poison gas they used,
To try to crush Sinn Fein,
And burnt our Irish capital,
Like the Germans did Louvain.

They shot our leaders in a jail,
Without a trial, they say,
They murdered women and children,
Who in their cellars lay,

And dug their grave with gun and spade,
To hide them from our view.
Because they could neither kill nor catch,
The rebel so bold and true.

The author should have sung that one.

PAT. That's if the thing has an author.

SOLDIER. Brendan Behan, he's too anti-British.

OFFICER. Too anti-Irish, you mean. Bejasus, wait till we get him back home. We'll give him what-for for making fun of the Movement.

SOLDIER [*to audience*]. He doesn't mind coming over here and taking your money.

PAT. He'd sell his country for a pint.

*What happens next is not very clear. There are a number of arguments all going on at once. Free-Staters against Republicans, Irish against English, homosexuals against heterosexuals, and in the confusion all the quarrels get mixed up and it looks as though everyone is fighting everyone else. In the centre of the mêlée, MISS GIL-CHRIST is standing on the table singing "Land of Hope and Glory". The I.R.A. OFFICER has one chair and is waving a Free State flag and singing "The Soldier's Song", while the RUSSIAN SAILOR has the other and sings the Soviet National Anthem. The NEGRO parades through the room carrying a large banner inscribed "KEEP IRELAND BLACK." The piano plays through out. Suddenly the VOLUNTEER attacks the SOLDIER and the RUSSIAN joins in the fight. The VOLUNTEER knocks MULLEADY's bowler hat over his eyes and ROPEEN flattens the VOLUNTEER. MULLEADY is now wandering around blind with his hat over his eyes, and holding*

ROPEEN's *aspidistra. The* VOLUNTEER, *somewhat dazed, sees the* RUSSIAN's *red flag and thinks he has been promoted to guard. He blows his railway whistle and the fight breaks up into a wild dance in which they all join on the train behind the* VOLUNTEER *and rush round the room in a circle. All this takes about a minute and a half and at the height, as they are all chugging round and round* LESLIE, PAT *interrupts.*

PAT. Stop it a minute. Hey, Leslie, have you seen this?

*The train stops and the dancers are left in the position of forming a ring round* LESLIE *which resembles a prison cage.* PAT *hands* LESLIE *a newspaper and everyone is quiet. The Irish, British, and Russian flags lie on the ground.*

SOLDIER. Let's have a look. "The Government of Northern Ireland have issued a statement that they cannot find a reason for granting a reprieve in the case of the condemned youth. The I.R.A. have announced that Private Leslie Alan Williams"—hey, that's me, I've got me name in the papers.

PAT. You want to read a bit further.

MISS GILCHRIST. I'm afraid it's impossible—you're going to be shot.

SOLDIER. Who are you?

MISS GILCHRIST. I am a sociable worker. I work for the St. Vincent de Paul Society and I have one question to ask you: have you your testament?

*The* SOLDIER *checks his trousers.*

SOLDIER. I hope so.

MISS GILCHRIST. I feel for him like a mother. [*She sings*].

　　Only a box of matches—

F

SOLDIER. Shut up, this is serious. "In a statement today delivered to all newspaper offices and press agencies—he has been taken as a hostage—If . . . executed—the I.R.A. declare that Private Leslie Alan Williams will be shot as a reprisal." Does it really mean they're going to shoot me?

MULLEADY. I'm afraid so.

SOLDIER. Why?

MONSEWER. You are the hostage.

SOLDIER. But I ain't done nothing.

OFFICER. This is war.

SOLDIER. Surely one of you would let me go?

*They all move backwards away from him, leaving him alone in the room. They disappear.*

Well, you crowd of bleeding—Hey, Kate, give us some music.

*He sings:*

I am a happy English lad, I love my royal-ty,
And if they were short a penny of a packet of fags,
Now they'd only have to ask me.

I love old England in the east, I love her in the west,
From Jordan's streams to Derry's Walls,
I love old England best.

I love my dear old Notting Hill, wherever I may roam,
But I wish the Irish and the niggers and the wogs,
Were kicked out and sent back home.

*A bugle sounds and he salutes.*

CURTAIN

# Act Three

*Late the same night. The* SOLDIER *sits alone in his room.*
PAT *and* MEG *sit at the table down by the piano.*
TERESA, COLETTE, RIO RITA *and* PRINCESS GRACE *are*
*sitting or sprawling on the stairs or in the passage.*
ROPEEN *sits, knitting, on a beer barrel near* PAT, *and the*
RUSSIAN *is fast asleep on the far side of the stage. Be-*
*fore the curtain rises there is the sound of keening as*
*the women sit mourning for* LESLIE *and the boy in*
*Belfast Jail. The atmosphere is one of death and dying.*
*The curtain rises and* PAT *seizes a bottle of stout from*
*the crate beside him and bursts into wild song:.*

PAT.　　　On the eighteenth day of November,
　　　　　Just outside the town of Macroom,

　　Here, have a drink. [*He gives* LESLIE *the stout.*]

SOLDIER. What's the time?

PAT. I don't know. Ask him.

VOLUNTEER. My watch has stopped.

PAT [*sings*].The Tans in their big Crossley tenders,
　　　　　Came roaring along to their doom.

MEG. Shut up, will you, Pat!

　　*The keening stops.*

PAT. What's the matter with you?

MEG. You'll have that Holy Joe down on us.

PAT. Who are you talking about?

79

MEG. That I.R.A. general, or whatever he is.

PAT. Him a general? He's a messenger boy. He's not fit to be a batman.

MEG. I've heard they're all generals nowadays.

PAT. Like their mothers before them.

> MISS GILCHRIST *in her nightclothes attempts to sneak into* LESLIE'S *room, but the* VOLUNTEER, *who is mounting guard, sees her and challenges.*

MISS GILCHRIST. Leslie—Leslie—

VOLUNTEER. Hey, where are you going?

PAT. Come on, come and sit down. [PAT *drags a protesting* MISS GILCHRIST *to sit at the table with them.*]

MISS GILCHRIST. Well, you must excuse the way I'm dressed.

PAT. You look lovely. Have a drink, Miss Gilchrist.

MISS GILCHRIST. Oh no, thank you, Mr. Pat.

PAT. Get it down you.

MISS GILCHRIST. No really, Mr. Pat. I never drink.

MEG. She doesn't want it.

PAT. Shut up, you. Are you going to drink?

MISS GILCHRIST. No, Mr. Pat.

PAT [*shouts*]. Drink. [*She drinks.*] Are you aware, Miss Gilchrist, that you are speaking to a man who was a commandant at the times of the troubles.

MEG. Fine bloody commandant he was.

PAT. Commandant of "E" battalion, second division, Dublin brigade. Monsewer was the Captain.

MEG. What the hell's "E" battalion?

PAT. You've heard of A B C D E, I suppose?

MEG. Certainly I have.

PAT. Well, it's as simple as that.

MISS GILCHRIST. Wasn't that nice? It must be a lovely thing to be a captain.

PAT. Can I get on with my story or not?

MEG. I defy anyone to stop you.

PAT. Now, where was I?

VOLUNTEER. Tell us about Mullingar, sir.

PAT. Shut up. Leslie, you want to listen to this. It was in Russell Street in Dublin—

MEG. That's my story and I've already told him.

PAT. Oh, then give us a drink.

MEG. Get it yourself.

PAT. Give us a drink!

    MISS GILCHRIST *gives* PAT *a drink*.

MISS GILCHRIST. Please go on, Mr. Pat.

PAT. I intend to. It was at Mullingar, at the time of the troubles, that I lost my leg . . .

MEG. You told me it was at Cork.

PAT. It doesn't matter what I told you, it was at Mullingar, in the Civil War.

MISS GILCHRIST. Well if that's the kind of war you call a civil war, I wouldn't like to see an uncivil one.

PAT. The fightin', Miss Gilchrist, went on for three days without ceasing, three whole days . . .

MISS GILCHRIST. And how did you lose your poor left foot, Mr. Pat?

PAT. It wasn't me left foot, but me right foot. Don't you know your left from your right? Don't you know how to make the sign of the cross?

MISS GILCHRIST. I do, thank you, but I don't make it with me feet.

> PAT *retreats to join* LESLIE *and the* VOLUNTEER *inside the room.*

PAT. What the hell difference does it make, left or right? There were good men lost on both sides.

VOLUNTEER. There's good and bad on all sides, sir.

> *The* I.R.A. OFFICER *crosses through the room and out again.*

PAT. It was a savage and barbarous battle. All we had was rifles and revolvers. They had Lewis guns, Thompsons, and landmines—bloody great landmines—the town was nothing but red fire and black smoke and the dead were piled high on the roads . . .

MEG. You told me there was only one man killed.

PAT. What?

MEG. And he was the County Surveyor out measuring the road and not interfering with politics one way or another.

PAT. You're a liar!

MEG. You told me that when the fighting was over both sides claimed him for their own.

PAT. Liar!

MEG. Haven't I seen the Celtic crosses on either side of the road where they both put up memorials to him?

PAT. It's all the same what I told you.

MEG. That's your story when you're drunk, anyway, and like any other man, that's the only time you tell the truth.

PAT. Have you finished?

MEG. No, begod, if whisky and beer were the prewar prices, the father of lies would be out of a job.

PAT. I lost my leg—did I or did I not?

MEG. You lost the use of it, I know that.

MISS GILCHRIST. These little lovers' quarrels.

PAT. Shut up! I lost my leg. Did I or did I not? And these white-faced loons with their berets and trench coats and teetotal badges have no right to call themselves members of the I.R.A.

MISS GILCHRIST. They're only lads, Mr. Pat.

MEG. He begrudges them their bit of sport now that he's old and beat himself.

PAT. What sport is there in that dreary loon out there?

MEG. They've as much right to their drilling and marching, their rifles and revolvers and crucifixes and last dying words and glory as ever you had.

PAT. I'm not saying they haven't, did I? [*There is general disagreement.*]

VOLUNTEER. Oh yes, you did, Pat.

MISS GILCHRIST. I heard you distinctly.

MEG. Weren't you young yourself once?

PAT. That's the way they talk to you, nowadays.

*He sulks. The keening starts again.*

MISS GILCHRIST. I always say that a general and a bit of shooting makes one forget one's troubles.

MEG. Sure, it takes your mind off the cost of living.

MISS GILCHRIST. A poor heart it is that never rejoices.

PAT. I'll tell you one thing, they've no right to be going up to

the border and kidnapping young men like this and bringing them down here.

MEG. They've as much right to leave their legs and feet up on
the border as ever you had at Mullingar or Cork or
wherever it was.

> MISS GILCHRIST *gets up to take a drink to* LESLIE. *The*
> VOLUNTEER *throws her out of the room.*

VOLUNTEER. I've warned you before you can't come in
here.

MEG. Leave her alone.

PAT. She's coming on, you know, to be making smart re-
marks to a poor crippled man that never harmed anyone
in his life.

MEG. Away with you.

PAT. Let alone the years I spent incarcerated in Mountjoy
with the other Irish patriots, God help me.

MEG. Ah, Mountjoy and the Curragh Camp were universi-
ties for the like of you. But I'll tell you one thing, and
that's not two, the day you gave up work to run this house
for Monsewer and take in the likes of this lot, you became
a butler, a Republican butler, a half-red footman—a Sinn
Fein skivvy—

MISS GILCHRIST, What a rough-tongued person.

PAT. Go on, abuse me, your own husband that took you off
the streets on a Sunday morning, when there wasn't a pub
open in the city.

MEG. Go and get a mass said for yourself. The only love you
ever had you kept for Mother Ireland and for leaving
honest employment.

PAT. Why did you stop with me so long?

MEG. God knows. I don't. God knows.

*On the stairs and in the passage people are dozing off.*
PAT *and* MEG *are not speaking. The* SOLDIER *is thinking
about tomorrow morning and to cheer himself up, sings.
The* I.R.A. OFFICER *passes on his rounds.*

SOLDIER. Abide with me, fast falls the eventide,
        The darkness deepens, Lord with me abide.

    MISS GILCHRIST *places a black lace scarf on her head,
lights a candle and starts walking slowly towards the*
SOLDIER, *keening. The* VOLUNTEER *is struck helpless.*

MEG. She's starting a wake for the poor lad and he's not
dead yet.

    *As she passes* PAT, *he blows out the candle and* MISS GIL-
CHRIST *suffers a great shock.*

PAT [*to* LESLIE]. If you must sing, sing something cheerful.

SOLDIER. I don't know anything cheerful.

VOLUNTEER. Then shut up!

    *Having got into the room,* MISS GILCHRIST *stays there.*

MISS GILCHRIST. I know what it is to be in exile. Dublin is
not my home.

MEG. That's one thing in its favour.

MISS GILCHRIST. I came here to work in a house, Mr. Pat.

MEG. I told you what she was.

MISS GILCHRIST. It was in a very respectable district. We
only took in clerical students. They were lovely boys, so
much more satisfactory than the medical students.

PAT. Oh yes, the medicals is more for the beer.

MISS GILCHRIST. Of course, my boys had renounced the
demon drink. Being students of divinity they had more
satisfactory things to do.

MEG. Such as?

PAT. You know what they go in for, reading all this stuff about "Mat begat Pat" and "This one lay with that one" and the old fellow that lay with his daughters—

MEG. And getting the best of eating and drinking, too. It's a wonder they're in any way controllable at all.

MISS GILCHRIST. Sometimes they were not. Life has its bitter memories. Since then I've had recourse to doing good works, recalling the sinner, salvaging his soul.

MEG. Well, you can leave his soul alone, whatever about your own, or I'll set fire to you.

MISS GILCHRIST [*standing on her dignity*]. Our Blessed Lord said, "Every cripple has his own way of walking, so long as they don't cause strikes, rob, steal, or run down General Franco." Those are my principles.

MEG. Your principal is nothing but a pimp.

MISS GILCHRIST. To whom are you referring?

MEG. That creeping Jesus on the third floor back.

MISS GILCHRIST. Oh, you mean Mr. Mulleady.

MEG. I do.

MISS GILCHRIST. But he is a fonctionnaire.

MEG. Is that what they call it nowadays?

MISS GILCHRIST. I strove to save him, together we wrestled against the devil, but here I feel is a soul worth the saving.

[*She sings*]. "I love my fellow creatures."

> MISS GILCHRIST *chases* LESLIE *round the table and the* VOLUNTEER *chases* MISS GILCHRIST.

PAT. Leave him alone, he's too young for you.

MISS GILCHRIST. Mr. Pat, I'm as pure as the driven snow.

*The* VOLUNTEER *taps her on the backside with his rifle.*
*She jumps.*

MEG. You weren't driven far enough.

MISS GILCHRIST *returns to the table near the piano.*

PAT. Hey, Feargus, Have a drink and take one up for
Leslie. Hey, Leslie, don't be paying any attention to her.
She's no use to you.

*The* VOLUNTEER *takes* LESLIE *a bottle of stout.*

SOLDIER. Here, it's all very well you coming the old acid,
and giving me all this stuff about nothing going to happen
to me, I'm not a complete bloody fool, you know.

PAT. Drink your beer and shut up.

SOLDIER. What have I ever done to you that you should
shoot me?

PAT. I'll tell you what you've done, Some time ago there
was a famine in this country and people were dying all
over the place. Well, your Queen Victoria, or whatever
her bloody name was, sent five pounds to the famine fund
and at the same time she sent five pounds to the Battersea
Dog's Home so no one could accuse her of having rebel
sympathies.

MEG. Good God, Pat, that was when Moses was in the Fire
Brigade.

PAT. Let him think about it.

MISS GILCHRIST. They might have given us this little island
that we live on for ourselves.

SOLDIER. Will you answer me one thing man to man? Why
didn't they tell me why they took me?

PAT. Didn't they? Didn't they tell you?

SOLDIER. No.

MEG. There's a war on.

PAT. Exactly. There's a war going on in the north of Ireland. You're a soldier. You were captured.

SOLDIER. All right, so I'm a soldier. I'm captured. I'm a prisoner of war.

PAT. Yes.

SOLDIER. Well, you can't shoot a prisoner of war.

PAT. Who said anything about shooting?

SOLDIER. What about that announcement in the newspapers?

PAT. Bluff. Haven't you everything you could wish for? A bottle of stout, a new girl-friend bringing you every class of comfort?

SOLDIER. Yeah, till that bloke in Belfast is topped in the morning; then it's curtains for poor old Williams. I'm due for a week-end's leave an' all.

PAT. It's bluff, propaganda! All they'll do is hold you for a few days.

MEG. Sure, they might give him a last-minute reprieve.

SOLDIER. Who, me?

MEG. No. The boy in Belfast Jail.

SOLDIER. Some hopes of that.

PAT. The British Government might think twice about it now that they know we've got you.

VOLUNTEER. They know that if they hang the Belfast martyr, their own man here will be plugged.

SOLDIER. Plug you.

PAT. Be quiet, you idiot.

*They all turn on the* VOLUNTEER.

SOLDIER. You're as barmy as him if you think that what's happening to me is upsetting the British Government. I suppose you think they're all sitting around in the West End clubs with handkerchiefs over their eyes, dropping tears into their double whiskies. Yeah, I can just see the Secretary of State for War now waking up his missus in the night: "Oh Isabel-Cynthia love, I can hardly get a wink of sleep wondering what's happening to that poor bleeder Williams."

MISS GILCHRIST. Poor boy! Do you know, I think they ought to put his story in the *News of the World*. Ah, we'll be seeing you on the telly yet. He'll be famous like that Diana Dors, or the one who cut up his victim and threw the bits out of an aeroplane. I think he has a serial running somewhere.

SOLDIER. I always heard the Irish were barmy, but that's going it, that is.

PAT. Eh, let's have a drink.

MEG. I want me bed, Pat. Never mind a drink.

SOLDIER. Here mum, listen—[*Coming out of the room.*]

PAT [*to the* SOLDIER]. Where are you going?

SOLDIER. I'm just going to talk to . . .

PAT. I'm going to fix you . . . Leslie.

MEG *starts to sing softly;*

"I have no mother to break her heart,
I have no father to take my part.
I have one friend and a girl is she,
And she'd lay down her life for McCaffery."

Now, I'm going to draw a circle round you, with this piece of chalk. Now, you move outside that circle and you're a dead man. Watch him, Feargus.

*He draws a circle round* LESLIE *and the* VOLUNTEER *points his gun at him.*

SOLDIER. I bet that fellow in Belfast wouldn't want me plugged.

PAT. Certainly he wouldn't.

SOLDIER. What good's it going to do him?

MEG. When the boy's dead, what good would it be to croak this one? It wouldn't bring the other back to life now, would it?

*The* VOLUNTEER *comes away from* LESLIE *to sit near the piano.*

SOLDIER. What a caper! I'm just walking out of a dance hall—

*He tries to walk out of the circle and the* VOLUNTEER *grabs his gun.*

PAT. Walk in.

SOLDIER [*back inside*]. I was just walking out of a dance hall, when this geezer nabs me. "What do you want?" I says. "Information," he says. "I ain't got no information," I says, "apart from me name and the addresses of the girls in the N.A.A.F.I." "Right," he says, "we're taking you to Dublin. Our Intelligence want to speak to you."

PAT. Intelligence! Holy Jesus, wait till you meet 'em. This fellow here's an Einstein compared to them.

SOLDIER. Well, when will I be meeting them?

PAT. Maybe they'll come tomorrow morning to ask you a few questions.

SOLDIER. Yeah, me last bloody wishes, I suppose.

MISS GILCHRIST [*sings*].

>I have no mother to break her heart,
>I have no father to take my part.

MEG. Pat, will you do something about that one?

PAT. Can you see that circle?

MISS GILCHRIST. Yes.

PAT. Well, get in.

>*He rushes* MISS GILCHRIST *into the room.*
>MISS GILCHRIST *carries on singing.*

MISS GILCHRIST.

>I have one friend, and a girl is she,
>And she'd lay down her life for McCaffery.

PAT. Leslie, come down here. That old idiot would put years on you. I can't stand your bloody moaning.

MISS GILCHRIST. I'll have you know, Mr. Pat, I had my voice trained by an electrocutionist.

MEG. It sounds shocking.

VOLUNTEER [*jumping to attention*]. Sir, it's neither this nor that, sir, but if you're taking charge of the prisoner, I'll carry out me other duties and check the premises.

PAT. Yes, you do that, Feargus.

VOLUNTEER. It's only a thick would let the job slip between his fingers.

PAT. You may be blamed, Einstein, but you never will be shamed.

VOLUNTEER. I hope not, sir. Of course, sir, God gives us the brains, it's no credit to ourselves.

PAT. Look—I don't wish to come the sergeant-major on you, but will you get about what you came for?

VOLUNTEER. I will, sir, directly.

*He salutes smartly and marches off into the growing dark,
getting more and more frightened as he goes.*

MISS GILCHRIST. I have such a thirst on me, Mr. Pat. [*She
looks at the crate of empties.*] Oh, Mr. Pat, you gave that
twelve of stout a very quick death.

PAT. You could sing that if you had an air to it. Leslie, pop
out and get us twelve of stout. Go on—just out there and
round the corner—go on—you can't miss it. Tell 'em it's
for me.

LESLIE *takes some persuading, but finally, seeing his
chance to escape, leaves quietly. Everyone else is falling asleep. There is a long silence, then a terrific
clatter.*

VOLUNTEER. Hey, where do you think you're going?

LESLIE. He told me I could . . .
LESLIE *runs back, hotly pursued by the* VOLUNTEER.
*Everyone wakes up in alarm.* PAT *is furious.*

VOLUNTEER. I caught the prisoner, sir, trying to escape.

PAT. You're a bloody genius, Einstein. [*The* VOLUNTEER
*beams.*] If you're so fond of that circle, you get in it. [*He
takes a swipe at the* VOLUNTEER *with his walking stick and
drives him into the circle. The* VOLUNTEER *is puzzled.*]
Leslie, come and sit over here.

LESLIE. Oh yeah, you're just leading me up the garden path,
sending me out for beer. All of a sudden, I turn round and
cop a bullet in my head. Anyway, I can tell you this, an
Englishman can die as well as an Irishman any day.

PAT. Don't give me all that old stuff about dying. You won't
die for another fifty years, barring you get a belt of an
atom bomb, God bless you.

LESLIE *comes down to sit with* PAT *and* MEG, *as* MONSEWER *enters at the back of the room with the* I.R.A. OFFICER. *The* VOLUNTEER *reports to them about the disturbance.*

MONSEWER. Have you checked his next-of-kin?

VOLUNTEER. He hasn't got none, sir.

*The* I.R.A. OFFICER *and* VOLUNTEER *synchronize watches and the* OFFICER *and* MONSEWER *depart. The* VOLUNTEER *sits at the table with his gun trained on* LESLIE'S *back.*

PAT. Come and sit down here and don't pay any attention to them.

MEG. Ignore them. Come on, lad.

SOLDIER. You know, up till tonight I've enjoyed myself here. It's better than square bashing. You know what they say? [*Sings.*]

> When Irish eyes are smiling,
> Sure, it's like a morn in Spring,
> In the lilt of Irish laughter
> You can hear the angels sing.
> When Irish eyes are happy—

*None of the Irish know the words, but they all hum and whistle.* MISS GILCHRIST *starts keening and the singing stops.*

PAT. It's all right, it's one of ours.

MISS GILCHRIST. Jesus, Mary and Joseph, I feel for this boy as if I were his mother.

MEG. That's remarkable, that is.

MISS GILCHRIST. It would be more remarkable if I were his father.

MEG. Were his father? How many of you are there? I never heard you were married.

MISS GILCHRIST. You never heard the Virgin Mary was married.

MEG. That was done under the Special Powers Act by the Holy Ghost.

MISS GILCHRIST. Oh, Miss Meg, I repulse your prognostications. It would answer you better to go and clean your carpet.

MEG. How dare you? When I was ill I lay prostituted on that carpet. Men of good taste have complicated me on it. Away, you scruff hound, and thump your craw with the other hippo-crites.

MISS GILCHRIST. Pray do not insult my religiosity.

MEG. Away, you brass.

MISS GILCHRIST. I stand fast by my Lord, and will sing my hymn now:

> I love my dear Redeemer,
> My Creator, too, as well,
> And, oh, that filthy Devil,
> Should stay below in Hell.
> I cry to Mr. Kruschev
> Please grant me this great boon,
> Don't muck about, don't muck about,
> Don't muck about with the moon.
>
> I am a little Christ-ian,
> My feet are white as snow,
> And every day, my prayers I say,
> For Empire Lamb I go.
> I cry unto Macmillan,
> That multi-racial coon,
> I love him and those above him,
> But don't muck about with the moon,

ALL. Don't muck about, don't muck about,
Don't muck about with the moon.

MEG. Get off the stage, you castle Catholic bitch.

MISS GILCHRIST. She is a no-class person. Things haven't been the same since the British went.

SOLDIER. They've not all gone yet—I'm still here. Perhaps you can tell me what these people are going to do me in for?

MEG. Maybe you voted wrong.

SOLDIER. I'm too young to have a vote for another three years.

MEG. Well, what are you doing poking your nose into our affairs?

SOLDIER. In what affairs? What do I know about Ireland or Cyprus, or Kenya or Jordan or any of those places?

OFFICER [*as he crosses the stage*]. You may learn very shortly with a bullet in the back of your head.

RIO RITA. You'll put a bullet in the back of nobody's head, mate.

WHORES. Oh no, it's not his fault.

MULLEADY. He should never have been brought here in the first place. It means trouble. I've been saying so all day. It's illegal.

*The action takes a very sinister turn. At the mention of bullets there is a rush by everyone to blanket* LESLIE *from the* OFFICER, MULLEADY *appears as if by magic and summons* RIO RITA *and* PRINCESS GRACE *to him. They go into a huddle. The other inhabitants of the house are mystified. All that can be seen are three pairs of twitching hips, as they mutter and whisper to each other.*

G

MEG. What are they up to?

PAT. I wouldn't trust them as far as I could fling them.

COLETTE. What are you up to?

RIO RITA. We've made a pact.

> *There is much homosexual by-play between* MULLEADY *and the two queers.*

COLETTE. What sort of a pact? Political or—?

MULLEADY. One might as well be out of the world as out of the fashion.

> MISS GILCHRIST *is horrified.*

MISS GILCHRIST. Eustace, what are you doing with those persons?

MULLEADY. Oh, we're speaking now, are we, Miss Gilchrist? That's a change. Ever since you've been interested in that young man's soul, a poor Civil Servant's soul means nothing to you.

MISS GILCHRIST. Eustace, what has happened to you?

MULLEADY. You can't do what you like with us, you know.

RIO RITA. Don't you know? [*He come down to the audience.*] Do you? Well, for the benefit of those who don't understand we'll sing our ancient song, won't we, Uncle? [MULLEADY *and* GRACE *join him.*] Blanche? [*This to the* NEGRO.] Isn't he lovely? I met him at a whist drive. He trumped my ace. Give us a note, Kate. Will you try another one, please? We'll have the first one, I think.

RIO RITA, MULLEADY, PRINCESS GRACE [*sing.*]

> When Socrates in Ancient Greece,
> Sat in his Turkish bath,
> He rubbed himself, and scrubbed himself,
> And steamed both fore and aft.

He sang the songs the sirens sang,
With Oscar and Shakespeare,
We're here because we're queer,
Because we're queer because we're here.

MULLEADY

The highest people in the land
Are for or they're against,
It's all the same thing in the end,
A piece of sentiment.

PRINCESS GRACE.

From Swedes so tall to Arabs small,
They answer with a leer,

ALL THREE.

We're here because we're queer
Because we're queer because we're here.

PRINCESS GRACE. The trouble we had getting that past the nice Lord Chamberlain. This next bit's even worse.

*The song ends and the three queers gyrate across the stage, twisting their bodies sinuously and making suggestive approaches to* LESLIE. LESLIE *is about to join in when* MISS GILCHRIST *throws herself at him.*

MISS GILCHRIST. Leslie, come away, this is no fit company for an innocent boy.

SOLDIER. No, mum.

MISS GILCHRIST. Leave off this boy. He's not used to prostitutes, male, female or *Whiston Mail.*

MEG. Get out, you dirty low things. A decent whore can't get a shilling with you around.

RIO RITA. Shut up, Meg Dillon, you're just bigoted.

MEG. Don't you use language like that to me.

MISS GILCHRIST. Leave off this boy. He is not a ponce.

SOLDIER. No, I'm a builder's labourer. At least, I was.

MISS GILCHRIST. Honest toil.

SOLDIER. It's a mug's game.

MISS GILCHRIST. Oh, my boy!

> *They sing a duet,* LESLIE *speaking his lines. As the song goes on, the whores and queers sort themselves out into a dance for all the outcasts of this world. It is a slow sad dance in which* ROPEEN *dances with* COLETTE *and* PRINCESS GRACE *dances first with* MULLEADY *and then with* RIO RITA. *There is jealousy and comfort in the dance.*

MISS GILCHRIST. Would you live on woman's earnings,
                Would you give up work for good?
                For a life of prostitution?

SOLDIER.        Yes, too bloody true, I would.

MISS GILCHRIST. Would you have a kip in Soho?
                Would you be a West End ponce?

SOLDIER.        I'm fed up with pick and shovel,
                And I'd like to try it once.

MISS GILCHRIST. Did you read the Wolfenden Report
                On whores and queers?

SOLDIER.        Yeah, gorblimey, it was moving,
                I collapsed meself in tears.

                Well, at this poncing business,
                I think I'll have a try,
                And I'll drop the English coppers,
                They're the best money can buy.

MISS GILCHRIST. Good-bye, my son, God bless you,
      Say your prayers each morn and night,
      And send home your poor old mother,
      A few quid—her widow's mite.

*At the end of the dance the* RUSSIAN *silently and smoothly removes* MISS GILCHRIST. *The whores and queers melt away, quietly cooing "Leslie!" There is a moment of stillness and quiet, when* TERESA *comes down into the darkened room and calls.*

TERESA. Leslie, Leslie!

*The* VOLUNTEER *is asleep at* LESLIE'S *table. He wakes up and sees* TERESA.

VOLUNTEER. You can call me Feargus! [*He leers lecherously.*]

PAT [*to* VOLUNTEER]. Hey, you'll have us all in trouble. Attention! Quick march—left, right, left, right . . . Come on, leave 'em in peace.

 PAT *throws out the* VOLUNTEER *and takes* MEG *away, to leave* LESLIE *alone with* TERESA.

TERESA. That strict officer is coming back and I won't get a chance of a word with you.

SOLDIER. Well, what do you want?

TERESA. Don't be so narky. I just wanted to see you.

SOLDIER. Well, you'd better take a good look, hadn't you?

TERESA. What's eating you? I only wanted to talk to you.

SOLDIER. You'd better hurry up, I mightn't be able to talk so well with a hole right through me head.

TERESA. Don't be talking like that.

SOLDIER. Why not? Eh, why not?

TERESA. Maybe I could get you a cup of tea?

SOLDIER. No, thanks, I've just had a barrel of beer.

TERESA. Well, I'll go then.

SOLDIER. Eh, just before you go, don't think you've taken me for a complete bloody fool, will you? All this tea and beer lark: you even obliged with that. [*Indicating the bed.*]

TERESA. Leslie, for God's sake! Do you want the whole house to hear?

LESLIE *takes her to the window.*

SOLDIER. Come here—I'll show you something. Can you see him over there, and that other one opposite? There are more than these two idiots guarding me. Look at those two, by the archway, pretending they're lovers. That should be right up your street, that, pretending they're lovers. That's a laugh.

TERESA. I wasn't pretending.

SOLDIER. How can I believe you, you and your blarney?

TERESA. The boys won't harm you. Pat told me himself; they only wanted to question you . . .

SOLDIER. Do you think he's going to tell you the truth, or me? After all—if you were really sorry for me, you might call the police. Well, would you, Teresa?

TERESA. I'm not an informer.

SOLDIER. How long have I got? What time is it?

TERESA. It's not eleven yet.

SOLDIER. Eleven o'clock. They'll just be waking up at home, fellows will be coming out of the dance halls.

TERESA [*still at the window*]. Look, there's an old fellow, half jarred, trying to sober up before he gets back home.

SOLDIER. Back home, couple of hundred miles away, might just as well be on another bloody planet.

TERESA. Leslie, the chip shop is still open, maybe I could go out—

SOLDIER. I couldn't eat chips. Could you eat chips if you knew you were going to be done in? You're thinking of that poor bloke in Belfast. What about me—here now, Muggins?

TERESA. If I really thought they'd do anything to you—

SOLDIER. If you thought—I'm a hostage. You know what that means? What's the point of taking a hostage if you don't intend to do him in?

TERESA. Leslie, If they do come for you, shout to me.

SOLDIER. Shout! I wouldn't get a chance.

TERESA. I can't be sure.

SOLDIER. Oh, go away and leave me in peace. At least that bloke in Belfast has peace, and tomorrow he'll have nuns and priest and the whole works to see him on his way.

TERESA. What do you want?

SOLDIER. Nothing—this bloke'll do the best he can on his own. Perhaps I'll meet that Belfast geezer on the other side. We can have a good laugh about it.

TERESA. Here's that officer coming. I'd better go.

*She starts to leave him.*

LESLIE [*frightened*]. Teresa! Don't go yet. I know I wasn't much good to you, but say good-bye properly, eh?

TERESA *goes to him and they clasp in each other's arms.*

If I get away, will you come and see me in Armagh?

TERESA. I will, Leslie.

SOLDIER. I want all the blokes in the billet to see you. They all got pictures on the walls. Well, I never had any pictures, but now I've got you. Then we could have a bloody good time in Belfast together.

TERESA. It would be lovely, astore.

SOLDIER. I'm due for a week-end's leave an' all . . .

TERESA. I could pay my own way, too.

SOLDIER. No, you needn't do that. I've got enough for both of us . . .

TERESA. They're coming.

PAT *and the* I.R.A. OFFICER *come down the stairs.*

OFFICER. What's she doing here? Sleeping with him?

PAT. Mind your own business. She's not interfering with you. You should be in bed now, girl. Where are you going?

TERESA. I'm just going to the chip shop, to get some chips for him.

*She starts to go, but the* OFFICER *stops her.*

OFFICER. You can't go out there now.

PAT. It's too late, girl.

TERESA. It's only eleven.

PAT. It's nearer one.

TERESA. It's not the truth you're telling me.

PAT. Didn't you hear the clock strike?

TERESA. I did.

OFFICER. Patrick, get her to her room or I will.

TERESA. You're lying to me. The chip shop is open till twelve.

OFFICER. Go to your room girl.

TERESA. Do I have to go?

PAT. Yes, go to your room.

> LESLIE *is left alone in his room until* MISS GILCHRIST *creeps from under the stairs to join him.*

MISS GILCHRIST. Oh, Leslie, what's going to become of you?

SOLDIER. I don't know, mum, do I?

MISS GILCHRIST. I've brought you a little gift. [*She gives him a photograph.*]

SOLDIER. Oh, she's nice!

MISS GILCHRIST. Oh, don't you recognize me, Leslie? It's me with me hair done nice.

SOLDIER. Oh, it's you. 'Ere, mum—I think you'd better go. Things might start warming up here.

MISS GILCHRIST. God go with you, Leslie. God go with you.

> *She goes*

SOLDIER [*to the audience*]. Well, that's got rid of her. Now the thing is will Teresa go to the cops? Even if old Einstein is half sozzled there's still the other two to get through. Will they shoot me? Yeah, I s'pose so. Will Teresa go to the cops? No.

> *There is an explosion which shakes the house and smoke wreathes the stage. Sirens blow, whistles scream and all the lights go out.* PAT *and* MEG *rush into the room and they and the* SOLDIER *hide behind the table. Pandemonium breaks out. What is actually happening is that* MULLEADY *has informed on* PAT *and* MONSEWER *and has brought the police to rescue* LESLIE. *He has*

*involved* RIO RITA *and* PRINCESS GRACE *in his schemes and they have corrupted his morals. The* RUSSIAN *has been a police spy all along. The police are now attacking the house and* MULLEADY *and* RIO RITA *are guiding them in.*

PAT. Take cover, there's a raid on.

MEG. I want to see what's going on.

PAT. Get your head down. They'll open fire any minute.

MULLEADY [*from the roof*]. Stand by. Two of you stay on the roof. The rest come down through the attic with me.

RIO RITA [*from the cellar*]. Six round the front, six round the back, and you two fellers follow me.

PAT. And take your partners for the eightsome reel. [*The piano plays.*]

MULLEADY. O'Shaunessy!

O'SHAUNESSY [*from the rear of the house*]. Sir!

MULLEADY. O'Shaunessy, shine a light for Jesus' sake.

O'SHAUNESSY [*off*]. I will, sir.

MULLEADY. Shine a light, I can't see a bloody thing.

O'SHAUNESSY [*off*]. I can't, sir, the battery's gone.

MULLEADY. To hell with the battery.

RIO RITA. Charge!

*His party go charging across the stage, but don't know where they're going or what they're doing. After confusion, they all charge back again.*

MULLEADY [*off*]. Right, down you go, O'Shaunessy.

O'SHAUNESSY. After you, sir.

MULLEADY. After you, man.

O'SHAUNESSY. After you, sir; I'm terrified of heights.

MULLEADY. Then close your eyes, man. This is war.

> *Pandemonium as the battle intensifies. Whistles and sirens blow, drums beat, bombs explode, bugles sound the attack, bullets ricochet and a confusion of orders are shouted all over the place. Bodies hurtle from one side of the stage to the other and, in the midst of all the chaos, the kilted figure of* MONSEWER *slow marches, serene and stately, across the stage, playing on his bagpipes a lament for the boy in Belfast Jail.* PAT *screams at him in vain.*

PAT. Sir! Sir! Get your head down. Get down, sir—there's a raid on. [*He touches* MONSEWER.]

MONSEWER. What? [*He stops playing and the din subsides.*]

PAT. There's a raid on.

MONSEWER. Then why the devil didn't you tell me? Man the barricades. Get the Mills bombs. Don't fire, laddie, till you see the whites of their eyes.

SOLDIER. I've only got a bottle.

MONSEWER. Up the Republic!

PAT. Get your head down, sir; they'll blow it off.

RIO RITA [*from under the stairs*]. Pat, do you want to buy a rifle?

PAT. Get out will you? [RIO RITA *goes.*]

> *The din subsides and the battle dies down. Inside the room are* MONSEWER, *in command,* PAT *by the window, and* MEG, COLETTE, ROPEEN *and* LESLIE *crawling round on the floor. Around the room the shadowy shapes of the forces of law and order flit in and out, darting across the stage and under the stairs.*

MONSEWER. What's happening, Patrick?

PAT. I'll just find out, sir. [*He looks out of the window and improvises a running commentary on the events outside.*] They're just taking the field. The secret police is ready for the kick off, but the regulars is hanging back. Mr. Mulleady has placed himself at the head of the forces of law and order and Miss Gilchrist is bringing up his rear. Princess Grace has joined the police . . . [*A whistle blows.*] The whistle's gone and they're off. [MULLEADY *crawls past the window on the window-sill.*] There's a man crawling along the gutter. He's going, he's going, he's gone! [*Crash of falling body, and a quarrel below.*]

SOLDIER. Teresa! Teresa! [*He thinks he's found her.*]

MEG. Shut up or I'll plug you, and your informer bitch when she comes in.

SOLDIER. Sorry, mum, I didn't know it was you.

> *There is an ominous silence. The piano is playing sinisterly.*

MONSEWER, Where's that officer chap?

PAT. I can't see him anywhere, sir.

MONSEWER. Do you mean to say he's deserted in the face of fire?

> *Suddenly a bugle sounds the attack. Figures run to take up positions surrounding the room.*

PAT. They're coming in.

MEG. Let's run for it.

MONSEWER. Hold fast!

PAT. I'm running. [*He runs.*]

MULLEADY. Halt, or I fire.

PAT. I'm halting. [*He stops with his hands up.*]

MONSEWER. Up the Republic!

SOLDIER. Up the Arsenal!

MULLEADY. Hands up, we're coming in.

MONSEWER. If you come in, we'll shoot the prisoner.

TERESA [*offstage*]. Run, Leslie, run.

> The SOLDIER *makes a break for it, zig-zagging across the stage, but every door is blocked. The drum echoes his runs with short rolls. As he makes his last run there is a deafening blast of gunfire and he drops.*

MULLEADY. Right, boys, over the top. [MULLEADY'S *men storm into the room and round up the defenders.* MULLEADY *is masked.*]

MONSEWER. Patrick, we're surrounded.

MEG [*to* PRINCESS GRACE]. Drop that gun or I'll kick you up the backside.

MONSEWER. Who are you?

MULLEADY. I'm a secret policeman and I don't care who knows it. [*He reveals himself. Two nuns scurry across the room and up the stairs, praying softly.*] Arrest those women. [*They are the two* I.R.A. *men in disguise.* TERESA *rushes into the room.*]

TERESA. Leslie! Leslie! Where's Leslie?
> *They all look around. No one has seen him.*

PAT. He was here a minute ago. [*He sees the body and goes down to it.*]

TERESA. Where is he ? Leslie. [*She sees him.*]

MEG. There he is.

PAT. He's dead. Take his identification disc.

RIO RITA [*kneeling to do it*]. I'll do it, sir. [*Finding the medal.*]
I didn't know he was a Catholic Boy.

TERESA. I gave it to him. Leave it with him.

MULLEADY. Cover him up.

> RIO RITA *covers the body with one of the nun's cloaks.*
> TERESA *kneels by the body. The others bare their*
> *heads.*

TERESA. Leslie, my love. A thousand blessings go with you.

PAT. Don't cry. Teresa. It's no one's fault. Nobody meant
to kill him.

TERESA. But he's dead.

PAT. So is the boy in Belfast Jail.

TERESA. It wasn't the Belfast Jail or the Six Counties that
was troubling you, but your lost youth and your crippled
leg. He died in a strange land, and at home he had no one.
I'll never forget you, Leslie, till the end of time.

> *She rises and everyone turns away from the body. A*
> *ghostly green light glows on the body as* LESLIE
> WILLIAMS *slowly gets up and sings:*

> The bells of hell,
> Go ting-a-ling-a-ling,
> For you but not for me,
> Oh death, where is thy sting-a-ling-a-ling?
> Or grave thy victory?
> If you meet the undertaker,
> Or the young man from the Pru,
> Get a pint with what's left over,
> Now I'll say good-bye to you.

*The stage brightens, and everyone turns and comes down
    towards the audience, singing:*

The bells of hell,
Go ting-a-ling-a-ling,
For you but not for him,
Oh death, where is thy sting-a-ling-a-ling!
Or grave thy victory.

CURTAIN

# *Methuen's Modern Plays*

### EDITED BY JOHN CULLEN AND GEOFFREY STRACHAN

Paul Ableman
*Green Julia*

Jean Anouilh
*Antigone*
*Becket*
*Poor Bitos*
*Ring Round the Moon*
*The Lark*
*The Rehearsal*
*The Fighting Cock*
*Dear Antoine*

John Arden
*Serjeant Musgrave's Dance*
*The Workhouse Donkey*
*Armstrong's Last Goodnight*
*Left-Handed Liberty*
*Soldier, Soldier and other plays*
*Two Autobiographical Plays*

John Arden and Margaretta D'Arcy
*The Business of Good Government*
*The Royal Pardon*
*The Hero Rises Up*

Ayckbourn, Bowen, Brook, Campton,
Melly, Owen, Pinter, Saunders, Weldon
*Mixed Doubles*

Brendan Behan
*The Quare Fellow*
*The Hostage*
*Richard's Cork Leg*

Barry Bermange
*No Quarter and The Interview*

Edward Bond
*Saved*
*Narrow Road to the Deep North*
*The Pope's Wedding*
*Lear*
*The Sea*

John Bowen
*Little Boxes*
*The Disorderly Women*

Bertolt Brecht
*Mother Courage*
*The Caucasian Chalk Circle*
*The Good Person of Szechwan*
*The Life of Galileo*
*The Threepenny Opera*

Syd Cheatle
*Straight Up*

Shelagh Delaney
*A Taste of Honey*
*The Lion in Love*

Max Frisch
*The Fire Raisers*
*Andorra*

Jean Giraudoux
*Tiger at the Gates*

Simon Gray
*Spoiled*
*Butley*

Peter Handke
*Offending the Audience and*
*    Self-Accusation*
*Kaspar*
*The Ride Across Lake Constance*

Rolf Hochhuth
*The Representative*

Heinar Kipphardt
*In the Matter of J. Robert Oppenheimer*

Arthur Kopit
*Chamber Music and other plays*
*Indians*

Jakov Lind
*The Silver Foxes are Dead and other*
*    plays*

David Mercer
*On the Eve of Publication*
*After Haggerty*
*Flint*

John Mortimer
*The Judge*
*Five Plays*
*Come As You Are*
*A Voyage Round My Father*
*Collaborators*

Joe Orton
*Crimes of Passion*
*Loot*
*What the Butler Saw*
*Funeral Games and*
*    The Good and Faithful Servant*
*Entertaining Mr Sloane*

Harold Pinter
*The Birthday Party*
*The Room and The Dumb Waiter*
*The Caretaker*
*A Slight Ache and other plays*
*The Collection and The Lover*
*The Homecoming*
*Tea Party and other plays*
*Landscape and Silence*
*Old Times*

David Selbourne
*The Damned*

Jean-Paul Sartre
*Crime Passionnel*

Wole Soyinka
*Madmen and Specialists*
*The Jero Plays*

Boris Vian
*The Empire Builders*

Peter Weiss
*Trotsky in Exile*

Theatre Workshop and Charles Chilton
*Oh What a Lovely War*

Charles Wood
*'H'*
*Veterans*

Carl Zuckmayer
*The Captain of Köpenick*